STONES TO Recovery

For Young People

Experience the miracle of 12 Step Recovery

Edited by Lisa D.

Seattle
Washington

Article Nos. 14, 95, 96, 120, © by The A.A. Grapevine, Inc.
Reprinted with permission.
Article Nos. 10, 52, 64, © by *The N.A. Way*. Reprinted with
permission.
Article No. 97, *Narcotics Anonymous*, 3d ed. rev. 1986, World
Service Office, Inc., p. 87.

Library of Congress Cataloging-in-Publication Data
Stepping stones to recovery : for young people / edited by Lisa D. — 1st
ed.
        p.   cm.
    Includes index.
    Summary: A guide and collection of readings for young people
involved in a twelve-step recovery program for an addiction. Includes
personal accounts of former drinkers and drug users.
    ISBN 0-934125-19-8 (pbk.) : $6.95
    1. Youth—Alcohol use. 2. Alcoholics—Rehabilitation. 3.
Twelve-step programs. 4. Youths' writings. [1. Alcoholics—Rehabilitation. 2. Narcotic addicts—Rehabilitation. 3. Alcoholism. 4. Drug
abuse. 5. Twelve-step programs.] I. D., Lisa.
HV5135.S75 1991
362.29'286'0835—dc20
                                                        91-8676
                                                        CIP
                                                        AC

First Edition
ISBN 0-934125-19-8
Printed in the United States of America

10 9 8 7 6 5 4

DEDICATED TO

All Young People
in 12 Step Recovery

PREFACE

This collection of personal stories, topical articles, slogans, prayers, and classic writings is for all young people recovering from addiction in one or any of the Twelve Step Fellowships. Many young people (13 to 25 years old) have helped me through interviews, comments, their writings, and submitting classic articles that have helped them. I am grateful to you all.

Young people in recovery, young people's groups, and treatment centers for young people are growing every year. We now understand that twenty-plus years of drinking or using, loss of family, job, and friends are not the only requirements to want recovery. We're never too young to be out of control and obsessed with the disease of alcoholism, drug addiction, dependencies, or compulsions. Young people in recovery know that their addiction could not be beaten with youth and the help they needed was waiting for them in 12 Step Programs.

This book focuses on the many issues important to young people who have begun recovery during adolescence or their early twenties.

The style and language of this book is written in a clear and "keep it simple" manner. Some words have been substituted so not to offend the reader. A daily reading guide is included for meditation. The message contained in these pages is that recovery, although not always easy, is rewarding.

A special thanks to my parents, Patti and Jerry, and my grandmother Eleanor, Stacey R., and Bruce G. for their love, support, and encouragement.

I had a wonderful time writing articles, editing, and compiling this collection and would like to thank Bill Pittman at Glen Abbey Books for believing in and guiding me through this project.

Most of all, I want to thank my Higher Power, whom I choose to call God, my fellow members, and the 12 Steps for showing me the way out of my addictions and helping me, as a young person, in recovery.

Lisa D.
Editor

CONTENTS

DAILY READING GUIDE

January

1. p.29 #17
2. p.102 #71
3. p.153 #107
4. p.7 #5
5. p.141 #98
6. p.56 #39
7. p.180 #124
8. p.168 #116
9. p.197 #136
10. p.34 #21
11. p.182 #126
12. p.73 #50
13. p.108 #77
14. p.216 #147
15. p.188 #131
16. p.47 #30
17. p.1 #1
18. p.121 #87
19. p.210 #145
20. p.25 #15
21. p.218 #150
22. p.62 #43
23. p.144 #101
24. p.126 #90
25. p.9 #8
26. p.90 #63
27. p.171 #118
28. p.49 #32
29. p.184 #128
30. p.98 #68
31. p.30 #18

February

1. p.81 #54
2. p.37 #23
3. p.167 #115
4. p.20 #14
5. p.172 #119
6. p.69 #47
7. p.106 #74
8. p.186 #130
9. p.8 #6
10. p.190 #133
11. p.114 #81
12. p.72 #49
13. p.18 #12
14. p.29 #16
15. p.53 #37
16. p.142 #99
17. p.152 #106
18. p.185 #129
19. p.6 #3
20. p.80 #53
21. p.150 #105
22. p.38 #24
23. p.146 #102
24. p.1 #2
25. p.163 #113
26. p.51 #35
27. p.86 #59
28. p.125 #89
29. p.9 #7

March

1. p.19 #13
2. p.120 #86
3. p.46 #29
4. p.160 #111
5. p.173 #120
6. p.71 #48
7. p.104 #73
8. p.118 #84
9. p.7 #4
10. p.203 #141
11. p.50 #33
12. p.90 #62
13. p.129 #92
14. p.31 #19
15. p.218 #149
16. p.100 #69
17. p.33 #20
18. p.117 #83
19. p.29 #17
20. p.96 #67
21. p.7 #5
22. p.54 #38
23. p.95 #66
24. p.84 #56
25. p.143 #100
26. p.113 #80
27. p.59 #42
28. p.17 #11
29. p.164 #114
30. p.188 #131
31. p.44 #28

DAILY READING GUIDE

	April		May		June
1.	p.40 #25	1.	p.35 #22	1.	p.59 #42
2.	p.74 #51	2.	p.115 #82	2.	p.108 #77
3.	p.149 #104	3.	p.161 #112	3.	p.146 #102
4.	p.87 #60	4.	p.50 #34	4.	p.50 #33
5.	p.169 #117	5.	p.183 #127	5.	p.81 #54
6.	p.52 #36	6.	p.95 #66	6.	p.163 #113
7.	p.192 #134	7.	p.177 #122	7.	p.178 #123
8.	p.216 #147	8.	p.42 #26	8.	p.53 #37
9.	p.43 #27	9.	p.198 #137	9.	p.103 #72
10.	p.85 #57	10.	p.89 #61	10.	p.19 #13
11.	p.176 #121	11.	p.123 #88	11.	p.188 #131
12.	p.110 #78	12.	p.9 #8	12.	p.18 #12
13.	p.12 #9	13.	p.199 #138	13.	p.114 #81
14.	p.131 #93	14.	p.58 #41	14.	p.78 #52
15.	p.34 #21	15.	p.85 #58	15.	p.188 #132
16.	p.137 #96	16.	p.128 #91	16.	p.48 #31
17.	p.13 #10	17.	p.6 #3	17.	p.96 #67
18.	p.73 #50	18.	p.72 #49	18.	p.51 #35
19.	p.106 #75	19.	p.206 #142	19.	p.217 #148
20.	p.30 #18	20.	p.29 #16	20.	p.7 #4
21.	p.101 #70	21.	p.98 #68	21.	p.197 #136
22.	p.1 #1	22.	p.181 #125	22.	p.29 #17
23.	p.63 #44	23.	p.56 #39	23.	p.102 #71
24.	p.202 #140	24.	p.201 #139	24.	p.8 #6
25.	p.49 #32	25.	p.82 #55	25.	p.207 #143
26.	p.119 #85	26.	p.107 #76	26.	p.218 #149
27.	p.217 #148	27.	p.104 #73	27.	p.90 #62
28.	p.57 #40	28.	p.9 #7	28.	p.134 #95
29.	p.218 #150	29.	p.144 #101	29.	p.196 #135
30.	p.48 #31	30.	p.91 #64	30.	p.37 #23
		31.	p.64 #45		

DAILY READING GUIDE

	July		August		September
1.	p.90 #63	1.	p.119 #85	1.	p.34 #21
2.	p.153 #107	2.	p.132 #94	2.	p.183 #127
3.	p.46 #29	3.	p.35 #22	3.	p.217 #148
4.	p.186 #130	4.	p.147 #103	4.	p.56 #39
5.	p.176 #121	5.	p.202 #140	5.	p.118 #84
6.	p.58 #41	6.	p.102 #71	6.	p.171 #118
7.	p.131 #93	7.	p.206 #142	7.	p.137 #96
8.	p.93 #65	8.	p.38 #24	8.	p.37 #23
9.	p.208 #144	9.	p.216 #147	9.	p.210 #145
10.	p.12 #9	10.	p.29 #16	10.	p.72 #49
11.	p.140 #97	11.	p.150 #105	11.	p.218 #149
12.	p.156 #109	12.	p.218 #150	12.	p.43 #27
13.	p.47 #30	13.	p.20 #14	13.	p.68 #46
14.	p.1 #1	14.	p.52 #36	14.	p.168 #116
15.	p.120 #86	15.	p.128 #91	15.	p.7 #4
16.	p.98 #68	16.	p.6 #3	16.	p.126 #90
17.	p.110 #78	17.	p.69 #47	17.	p.158 #110
18.	p.7 #5	18.	p.63 #44	18.	p.50 #34
19.	p.106 #74	19.	p.13 #10	19.	p.8 #6
20.	p.111 #79	20.	p.184 #128	20.	p.141 #98
21.	p.33 #20	21.	p.30 #18	21.	p.87 #60
22.	p.142 #99	22.	p.185 #129	22.	p.25 #15
23.	p.190 #133	23.	p.1 #2	23.	p.81 #54
24.	p.17 #11	24.	p.74 #51	24.	p.167 #115
25.	p.117 #83	25.	p.73 #50	25.	p.57 #40
26.	p.173 #120	26.	p.9 #7	26.	p.59 #42
27.	p.31 #19	27.	p.106 #75	27.	p.40 #25
28.	p.210 #145	28.	p.154 #108	28.	p.48 #31
29.	p.121 #87	29.	p.86 #59	29.	p.47 #30
30.	p.54 #38	30.	p.71 #48	30.	p.180 #124
31.	p.49 #32	31.	p.44 #28		

DAILY READING GUIDE

1. RECOVERY IS . . .

Recovery is the most important thing in our lives, without exception. We may believe our job, or our home life, or one of many other things comes first. But consider: if we don't stay with the Program, chances are we won't have a job, a family, sanity, or even life. If we are convinced that everything in life depends on our recovery, we have a much better chance of improving our lives. If we put other things first, we are only hurting our chances.

2. ONE OF THE YOUNG ONES

I did not drink for twenty years. I have never been to jail. I did not lose a wife, or a family. I did lose lots of jobs, lots of friends, a fair amount of weight, a good portion of my mind, and all of my self-respect. I lost quite enough. I was nineteen years old when I arrived at the doors of Alcoholics Anonymous; I was ready. I weighed 117 pounds. I was in active ketosis, I suffered from malnutrition, I had abscesses up and down my arms and legs. I had to puke up three or four shots of vodka every morning before I could get one down. I tried, desperately, a hundred times to stop drinking, to stop using, to stop destroying myself with chemicals. I am a survivor of eight suicide attempts. I am a drunk driver, a blackout driver, a liar, a cheat, and a thief.

"We could increase the list . . ." *ad nauseam.* The point is: I earned my seat in this Fellowship. I belong here. There is no doubt in my mind that I am an alcoholic. No denial. No reservations. No question. I drank and used for a little over seven years. I suppose that I drank my fill, that I drank hard enough and long enough to become teachable. I got here in time; one more shot of vodka swigged straight from the bottle and I might well have died.

When I first stumbled up the stairs of that miraculous place that was to become my home group in September 1986, I was the youngest drunk in sight. For the first few fogged months that hardly mattered. I was a newcomer and so I got lots of attention. I was also the resident young person, the token teenager. Everybody, and I mean everybody, wanted to talk to me.

Now I am one of them good drunks. You know the type: egocentric with an inferiority complex. I ate it up. I heard lots of good stuff, the words that saved my life and laid a strong foundation for me. I began to feel accepted and "a part of" for the first time in my life. I also heard countless times how lucky I was, how fortunate it was that I did not have to go through the things that "you people" went through. I, apparently, was spared your pain.

At first I thought I misunderstood you, or that you misunderstood me. I couldn't see how you could listen to my litany of woes, my incoherent babblings, my suicidal ranting, my anger, and my fear, and tell me I was lucky. I certainly did not feel lucky.

Of course, today I no longer believe in luck, just as I no longer believe in coincidences. Today I believe in miracles—I have to. My sobriety cannot be explained any other way. But I still feel that familiar knot in my gut, that tensing in my shoulders when someone tells me how lucky I am that I found the program at the age of nineteen, or when I hear some well-meaning soul expressing amazement and wonder at the influx of young people and expounding on how wonderful that a fifteen-year-old can arrest his disease at that age. It is equally wonderful when an old person finds sobriety, or a middle-aged person, or any kind of person. We know that alcoholism is no respecter of age or race or religion. And just as the disease cuts across social and economic barriers, so does the prospect of recovery.

Please do not minimize my pain. I got to this program out of utter desperation. I did not get here to hang out with you people and have a good time (although I have hung out with you people and had a great time). I did not get here because I thought I might be a "potential alcoholic" or because I saw the end in sight. I was at the end. I am not here because I am lucky. I am here by the grace of God, for the very same reason that you are here—because I'm a drunk, and a dope fiend, and I don't want to die.

Then . . . I heard myself . . . .

When I was sixty days sober and still fairly shaky, an older gentleman with a good many years of sobriety took me aside after a meeting. I heard one more time how lucky I was not "to have to go through what he had to go through." Well folks, that was it. That was the last straw. I called that good man every name in the book, and began a quest for young people's meetings. Chronic complainer that I was, I went to half a dozen meetings, complaining about those "old . . .s" the whole way. Finally, one day in my third month of sobriety, I happened upon a young people's meeting a few miles from my home group. There were maybe twelve or thirteen people there, median age fifteen. I was the oldest person in the room. I listened in amazement to their stories of their recovery, their boundless hope born out of fear and desperation. My mouth fell open in disbelief when I heard a fifteen-year-old girl share, liberally quoting the Big Book and glowing from the eyes. She had over a year of sobriety!

My God: Fifteen and a year! How glorious, I thought; she'll never have to go through the horrors I had to go through. She'll never know my pain.

It came time for me to share.

"My name is M. I am an alcoholic. And I've got to tell you how lucky you are . . . ." This all came out before my teeth came crashing down on my tongue. Thankfully, I shut my mouth. So you see, for all my preaching, even I was not immune.

I speak for myself, of course, but I must presume (Who, me? Arrogant?) that I speak for many of us younger AAs. *We are no different than you. We suffered too. We have earned our chairs in Alcoholics Anonymous.* Please don't tell us how lucky we are, lest you encourage us to go back out there and find out for ourselves. Please don't tell us how lucky we are, lest you set us apart and make us feel different, when what we need most is to feel the same.

Please don't tell us how lucky we are, unless you understand that you are "lucky," too.

3. SIGNS OF A SPIRITUAL AWAKENING

- ✓ An increased tendency to let things happen rather than make them happen.
- ✓ Frequent attacks of smiling.
- ✓ Feelings of being connected with others and nature.
- ✓ Frequent overwhelming episodes of appreciation.
- ✓ A tendency to think and act spontaneously rather than on fears based on past experience.
- ✓ An unmistakable ability to enjoy each moment.
- ✓ A loss of ability to worry.
- ✓ A loss of interest in conflict.
- ✓ A loss of interest in interpreting the actions of others.
- ✓ A loss of interest in judging others.
- ✓ A loss of interest in judging self.

4.   GOODBYE ADDICTION

Goodbye to the one I was going to spend my life with. The one I was willing to take for better or worse. The one with whom I was going to share my anger, resentment, self-pity, and self-centered egotism. The one that made me forget the pain of rejection, the feelings of worthlessness, and the memory of the hurt I caused myself and others. You let me down when I needed you most. Now I can do the things you told me I didn't need to do. With you gone, I can start the emotional and spiritual growth that you stopped when I started using. Goodbye, Addiction.

5.   CROSS TO BEAR

The young man was at the end of his rope. Seeing no way out, he dropped to his knees in prayer and said, "Lord, I can't go on. I have too heavy a cross to bear."

"My son," the Lord replied, "if you can't bear its weight, just place your cross inside this room and then open that other door and pick out any cross you wish."

"Thank you, Lord! Thank you!" the young man said in relief, and did as he was told.

Upon entering the other door he saw many crosses, some so large he couldn't see their tops. Finally he spotted a tiny cross leaning against the far wall. He said, "Lord, I'd like that one over there."

"My son," the Lord replied, "that is the cross you just brought in."

6.   TAKING CARE OF MYSELF 2/9/17

Learning to take care of myself is one of the valuable lessons I've learned in recovery. There were so many layers of junk I had to peel away before I understood this. At first taking care of myself meant just not picking up. Then I learned about H.A.L.T.—don't get too "Hungry, Angry, Lonely, or Tired." Taking care of myself means attending to my needs, instead of suffering, because when I take care of my basic needs I am less vulnerable to screwing up my recovery.

Taking care of myself has meant going to meetings, even when others would rather have me stay at home or do something else. I go to meetings because I always feel better after the meeting. I've learned to like feeling good.

Recently, I've learned that taking care of myself means doing something nice for myself. I guess that before coming to the Program, I just didn't think I was worth taking care of, or I didn't know how to do it. Now, I think I'm worth it and I'm learning how to do it.

7.   RESENTMENT HURTS

Resentment is the wound that never heals. And if I hold a resentment, it is I who am wounded. The person or persons I resent OWN me. They control my thoughts and my feelings—and ultimately my actions. It's my choice whether or not to "let it go" and get on with my life. The most basic level of forgiveness is the decision to "let it go." I choose other priorities. God willing, I may some-day be so serene and so adult and so sober that I can forgive myself or another the way God would do it—unconditionally and absolutely. Meanwhile, I'm free!

8.   DROP THE ROCK

Seems there was this group of 12 Step members taking a boat ride to this island called SERENITY, and they were truly a happy bunch of people. As the boat pulled away from the dock, a few on board noticed Mary running down the street trying to catch up with the boat. One said, "Darn, she's missed the boat." Another said, "Maybe not. Come on, Mary! Jump in the water! Swim! Swim! You can make it! You can catch up with us!"

So Mary jumped into the water and started to swim for all she was worth. She swam for quite a while, and then started to sink. The members on board, now all aware that Mary was struggling, shouted, "Come on, Mary! Don't give up! Drop the rock!" With that encouragement, Mary started swimming again, only to start sinking again shortly afterward. She was going under when she heard all those voices shouting to her, "Mary, drop the rock! Let go, and drop the rock!"

Mary was vaguely aware of something around her neck, but she couldn't quite figure out what it was. Once more, she gathered her strength and started swimming. She was doing quite well, even gaining a little on the boat, but then she felt this heaviness pulling her under again. She saw all those people on the boat holding out their hands and hollering for her to keep swimming and shouting, "Don't be an idiot, Mary! Drop the rock!"

Then she understood, when she was going down for the third time. This thing around her neck, *this* was why she kept sinking when she really *wanted* to catch the boat. This thing was the "rock" they were all shouting about: resentments, fear, dishonesty, self-pity, intolerance and anger, just some of the things her "rock" was made of. "Get rid of the rock," she told herself. "Now! Get rid of it!"

So Mary managed to stay afloat long enough to untangle a few of the strings holding that rock around her neck, realizing as she did that her load was easing up; and then, with another burst of energy, she let go. She tore the other strings off and dropped the rock.

Once free of the rock, she was amazed how easy it was to swim, and she soon caught up with the boat. Those on board were cheering for her and applauding and telling her how great she was, and how it was so good having her with them again, and how now we can get on with our boat ride and have a nice time.

Mary felt great and was just about to indulge in a little rest and relaxation when she glanced back to shore. There, a ways back, she thought she saw something bobbing in the water, so she pointed it out to some others. Sure enough, someone was trying to catch the boat, swimming for dear life but not making much headway. In fact, it looked like they were going under.

Mary looked around and saw the concern on the faces of the other members. She was the first to lean over the rail and shout, "Hey, friend! Drop the rock!"

9.   NEVER HAD A CHANCE

Yes, I'm an alcoholic, addict, overeater—you name it. I also grew up in an abusive alcoholic home. I've been in recovery now for four years, clean and sober and being consistent in eating the right foods.

Some information I received early on in recovery has been a help to me. Because of some genetic or other imbalance in my brain, I guess I never had a chance at being "normal." One can read extensively on this subject (most commonly called the "X Factor") or talk to experts, but they're a long way from finding the exact factors in the brain that make some of us susceptible to addiction.

This knowledge helped me get out of the shame and stop blaming myself for all the negative events in my life. I do remind myself that I have responsibility for some of the things that went on. Gradually, in early recovery, I began to accept my disease and became willing to do my best to live a different life; basically, I learned to know the difference between what's right or wrong, good or bad for me.

Perhaps I never had a chance to be "normal," but the Program and other help available has given me an opportunity to be a better me. I know I am less depressed when I eat right, lay off the sugar, and get a little exercise. I've learned to trust again, first the Program, then other people. The Eighth and Ninth Steps have helped me forgive my father for his abuse.

It's been very hard work at times, but the Steps and my fellow members have pulled me through. This *is* a better way to live.

10. NEVER TOO YOUNG TO DIE

I'm a very grateful recovering addict. My story probably doesn't differ much from anyone else's but I feel the need to share some of my experience, strength, and hope to encourage others.

I believe I was an addict before I ever picked up drugs, because I never fit in anywhere, though I certainly tried. I'd pretend to be different people. Wherever I was, I changed to be like the people I was with, all the time feeling like I had to prove myself.

I never felt loved or wanted. I tried to make people love me. I would make people write "I love you" down on a piece of paper and keep it in my wallet as "proof." I felt so unloved. I'd do insane things for attention. Once I slit my wrists in school. I didn't want to die, I just wanted to hurt myself bad enough so someone would come visit me in the hospital and pay some attention to me.

It felt like I fought for years for love and affection. After so long, I gave up. I took the attitude that I don't need anyone. I could do everything on my own and didn't want anyone to be around me. I didn't need you. I acted like nothing bothered me. I could handle everything. No one was going to get the best of me ever again.

Little did I know drugs eased that pain. Pretty soon there weren't enough drugs in the world to ease all the pain and rejection I felt. I had to stay numb twenty-four hours a day, seven days a week. I hated myself, I had no self-worth, self-respect or self-esteem. I allowed people to treat me like dirt, because I figured it was better than having no one at all.

I moved out of my dad's home when I was fifteen. I was determined to be "free." I didn't realize I was already in prison. I locked myself in a world of games and lies with fake people and false places. I always talked about all the places I'd go and all the things I'd do, but I always wound up in the same place doing the same thing, getting high. I was all talk.

I moved from place to place, always running, always trying to find happiness.

Using progressed—I stole and lied so much I began to believe my own lies. I was a "professional" when it came to making people feel sorry for me.

When I turned seventeen, I had a $300-a-day habit. I couldn't smoke enough coke, or anything else for that matter. I got into a car accident and then started having convulsions.

I've been to three treatment programs before I learned I'd never get help until I helped myself. I changed a lot since then. I used to think I was too young to die, too young to have a problem. Hogwash.

I surrendered and became willing to do anything it took. I have a great sponsor today, more friends that truly love me than I ever imagined. I work the Steps to the best of my ability. I have happiness in my life. No more clinging to my old image—I've found self-respect, self-worth, and (a little more) self-esteem.

I hold my head up high today because I'm worth something. I love myself. I speak at jails and treatment centers. I sponsor two women, and I'm involved in service work. It's so great to truly be free. I have real fun today, dancing and going to conventions.

I'm truly a miracle. I've never been so happy in my life. In four days I'll be nineteen, and in two more months I'll be celebrating my first year. I know I have a life-and-death disease. This is no game. I have a real patient monkey on my back waiting to kill me. But I choose life today.

Please don't ever give up on anyone. I was the one they said would never make it. But because you people loved me when I could not love myself, and you people didn't give up on me when I gave up on myself, I live today.

I could never thank you all enough for your help. I owe Narcotics Anonymous everything. I will be forever in debt to this program. Thank you, N.A., for my life.

I *am* too young to die. "My gratitude speaks . . . when I care and when I share with others the N.A. way."

11. ACCEPTANCE OF OURSELVES

Upon walking into these rooms, most of us knew very little about ourselves, much less accept ourselves for what we really were. Our egos told us "There's nothing wrong with me—everyone else is screwed up."

As we work the Steps we begin to see what we're really like and see selfishness, dishonesty, and other forms of our self-centered fear. We don't particularly like what we learn about our character and hit a brick wall. Will we accept the truth and work on our defects or will we stop looking because it's too painful?

Acceptance helps us work through denial, bargaining, anger, and depression. We deny there's anything wrong with us until it becomes too painful to blame the world and everyone in it for our trouble—we're forced to admit there's something wrong with us— not them. We try to bargain away what we don't like: "I wouldn't be so angry if you'd give me what I want, God." And anger shows itself—who would dare suggest we're less than perfect?   Our anger turns inward and becomes depression: "Poor me, my life isn't worth living because I've got some things wrong with me."

In the Program there is hope and a Step to work. No one ever said it was easy—accepting the truth has nothing to do with liking it—but if we try, we'll be a lot better than we used to be!

12. FREEDOM OF ACCEPTANCE

Third Step: *Made a decision to turn our will and our lives over to the care of God as we understood Him.*

One of the big problems we have is a denial of all kinds of feelings. We don't want to look at what we see on the dark side of ourselves. They are the things we hide and spend a lot of our precious energy keeping hidden. We hide things and keep people away from us so they won't see the skeletons in our closet. There also can be a great denial of our feelings of anger and pain when we try to achieve peace. Surrender helps us in all this, by letting us accept all the things in us and around us as they are. We give up the struggle against the world, and then we are free to change the few things about us that we can change, that really need changing.

We like acceptance, and the best way I've found to get acceptance is to give it first. Then I usually find I get back the acceptance I need.

Another thing I, or we, need to look at is surrender itself, so we can get a better understanding of that process. What is surrender? Is it ego or surrender? Living in ego means wanting what you don't have. Surrender means appreciating and being grateful for what you do have. Ego is when we constantly think we know what is best for us.

Surrender is when we see that the great stream of life, our Higher Power, or God as we understand Him, knows what is best for us. It is the prayer of release. Living the surrendered life is like being a butterfly, a soul in full flight seeking the beauties of life. Like the butterfly, we start putting our trust in the present good things instead of hoping for the next good thing. To get this attitude we need to seek a new vision, a new hope, a new spirit.

13. OUTLOOK OF TWO MEMBERS

Don D. went to a meeting one evening. He frowned when a member mispronounced a few words while reading "How It Works." He felt appalled when another member stood up and said he was an alcoholic and an addict. Another person talked too long. As he slipped out the door immediately after the meeting, he muttered, "That was terrible. I should have stayed home."

Bob M. went to a meeting one evening. His head was bowed as he listened to the "Preamble" and "How It Works." His eyes moistened as he listened intently to a member tell his story. He was grateful for being able to attend this meeting. After clean-up and a little socializing, he paused, and as he locked the meeting room door, his thoughts were, "Thank God for such a beautiful fellowship."

Both members were at the same meeting. Each found what they were looking for.

14. ROCK 'N ROLL SOBRIETY

I was very apprehensive but decided to loosen up a bit and go to the rock concert anyway. I felt I had grown out of a lot of that loud, deafening music, but since my sister really wanted me to go I agreed. What the hell, I was still young—twenty-three years old that is, and flexible enough to fit in with just about any group of people. I decided to make it a good time so I threw out my negative feelings and geared myself with a positive attitude. Thus was my mental state when I headed for the stadium to rock with the band.

We got there early enough to get good seats, and I sat back to observe the crowd of people that filed past. Their eyes sparkled with anticipation and their faces gave evidence of the excitement they felt. Raw energy hung low like a heavy fog and mixed with the warm, damp air left over from the muggy day. Multicolored, greased-up hair, six-inch chain earrings, black leather studded outfits, and bright, bold, colorful sunglasses caught my eye. Nothing was unexpected, however. I was merely a spectator enjoying the show as my continuous grin would suggest to those passing by.

The concert was finally getting under way and my friends needed more beer, so off they trotted to battle the crowds and long lines while I attempted to save their seat. Of course they missed the first song, and almost lost their seats. While I was dancing and clapping to the music I could see them off in the distance as they jostled their way through the crowd, trying to save their sacred beer from spillage. It seemed an eternity, but everyone finally settled in.

By this time the band was working up a sweat and the crowd's intense energy was growing. It didn't take long before the familiar smell of marijuana played on my senses. Oh, God! I decided right then and there to thank God for my sobriety. It seemed only yesterday when at this same concert

I was too stoned to even realize what songs were played. Hard rock is tough to figure out anyway, yet at least tonight my mind was intact and I could actually distinguish one instrument from the next and figure out the rhythm.

Unfortunately my enthusiastic, absorbed state was interrupted. "What d'ya want?" I screamed at my sister over the grating sound of heavy metal.

"We have to go to the bathroom," she yelled. I had forgotten that wretched curse of beer drinking.

"Okay," I shouted, "but hurry back. I can't be saving seats all night." Off they went again while I continued to enjoy the show. Yes, by God, I was enjoying this concert.

All around me people were losing their balance and falling off benches because of the effects of alcohol and drugs. Yet I firmly held my ground and confidently stepped up my movements in the tiny spot I inhabited. I was amazed at the amount of control I felt amid all this unleashed energy. Sweating bodies were pushed and shoved in the whirlwind of mass chaos, while endless screaming mingled in the air with pounding drums and electrifying acoustics—still, I was in control! My thoughts were soon disturbed by the scrawny kid next to me.

"Do you have an extra joint?"

"What?" I exclaimed, clearly flabbergasted. He was maybe fifteen or sixteen.

"Do you have any extra weed, man?" he repeated, somewhat hesitant this time.

"I wouldn't even have a match to light one for you," I answered. He didn't seem to believe me, but I really couldn't help him. I looked at him again and smiled.

Half an hour passed before I saw the familiar faces of my sister and her friends. They were having trouble getting through the wild crowd. Too bad they were missing the whole show. When they finally made it, I informed her that they had played her favorite song. "Don't go to the bathroom," she shouted in my ear, uninterested in my comment. "You wouldn't believe how long the lines are."

As she continued to be preoccupied with lighting her cigarette and carefully guarding what beer she had salvaged, I absorbed myself in the excitement of the live music and the fact that I was seeing—really seeing—a concert for the first time.

The thoughts and emotions that coursed through me that night are almost inexpressible. I recognized a year and a half of growth amid the blaring, screeching, deafening sounds of electric guitars and synthesizers, and saw for the first time that this was what self-esteem was all about. I was not afraid to do my own thing in this crowd. I was not worried about how I looked, nor intimidated by how others looked. I was not comparing myself to others; I was not crazy, and felt no need to act crazy; I was definitely not unhappy; and I was not thirsting for attention and acceptance, or trying so hard to feel that I belonged. I was not inside looking out; rather I was outside looking in.

I stood in the middle of 35,000 people and felt free to be a different, unique individual. The most important part of it all is that my Higher Power was with me and I was conscious of him. How many other people in this rowdy, rambunctious crowd were thinking of a God and feeling the greater effects of his energy and power? How many times while I was drinking did I become conscious of my Higher Power and my inner feelings? I can't think of one. The only times I remember being aware of that is when I cried out in pain and desperation. He was there then, but I couldn't see him through my tears, my darkness, my raw pain.

"Did you have a good time?" I asked my sister when it was all over.

"Yeah, it was great," she answered, but quickly changed the subject to the amount of beer that was spilled on her. I could plainly see the effects of the concert were short-lived. Tomorrow she would not remember the real music, only a loud, undistinguishable sound and a lot of people. I, however, had discovered a new dimension to my sobriety, and it was well worth a hard-earned six bucks!

15. YEAH, BUT . . .

As my five-year anniversary draws near, I feel not only grateful, but also overwhelmed. I walked into my first meeting six years ago looking to be taught how to drink the right way. Little did I know all the YETs that could happen only in a year: morning drinking, blackouts, lying and using people, dropping classes in college, people covering for me at work. Physically I had developed an enlarged liver that caused more pain than I could stand.

Worse than all those things were the feelings of self-hate, the fears, the suicidal thoughts, and so on. For a year I went to meetings but never put the drink down for more than four or five weeks at a time.

Almost a year later to the date, I had what I hoped was my last drink. How, at age twenty-one, could alcohol have taken control of my life? It didn't matter though, because it had.

That was almost five years ago, and by the grace of God, I am still sober today. My first two years in the Program were very difficult. I had constant depressions and suicidal thoughts, and constantly battled the desire to drink. After two years I ended up in a treatment center, luckily before I drank. I spent three weeks there, and it gave me a chance to take a better look at my sobriety.

I did not come out of the treatment center raring to go at the Program. The following two months I stayed on the fence and finally came close to drinking again. I had a sponsor, but now I started to really use her. One of the toughest things for me was to go to discussion meetings, but I went because my sponsor told me to go. For three months I said nothing more than my name and that I'm an alcoholic. But at least I went, and more important than that, I listened. I started hearing things for the first time, though I'm sure they had been said at meetings many times before. Little by little, changes were starting to take place, and a bit of honesty started developing.

What I began to realize was that I really was a lot like everybody else. I was sick, not bad. I started sharing a few thoughts and people were very patient with me. Eventually the fear of sharing started to decrease.

These last three years have been very different from the first two. There has been a lot of struggle, with ups and downs, bouts with depression, defiance, and taking control. But what I have learned not to do is keep it inside, because that only makes me sicker.

Looking back at those first two years, I see now why it was so difficult for me. I was loaded with anger, resentment, self-pity, jealousy; the list goes on. I worked hard at being who I thought everybody wanted me to be, happy-go-lucky without a care in the world, but inside I was falling apart. My acceptance of life and situations always had an *as long as* attached. I could turn my will and life over *as long as* . . . . I fought life every step of the way.

I used the program the way I used alcohol and drugs. I thought if I went to meetings (which I did), if I didn't drink (which I didn't), every day should be pain-free. When it didn't turn out that way, I became angry, resentful, full of self-pity, and didn't think the Program really worked. I hadn't dealt with feelings and emotions when I was drinking, and I wasn't dealing with them sober. But the Program started working for me when I started meeting life on life's terms and not my own.

I still go to five or six meetings a week—open, discussion, and Step meetings. The Steps are so important as I travel along the road to recovery. They help me with choices and decisions that have to be made day by day.

I am not alone any more unless I choose to be. The relationship I have developed with my Higher Power, whom I choose to call God, is unbelievable, and it can only get better as long as I keep doing what the Program suggests. I used to think that the less help I had to ask for, the better I was, because it meant I could do more on my own. I see where that kind of thinking led me. I ask for help a lot today, not only in the morning and at night, but also throughout the day.

In order for me to maintain my sobriety and serenity, to live life the way it is supposed to be lived, I need total reliance on God, sharing what is going on in my life with other people, and doing what I am supposed to do no matter how I feel.

16. REBELS

I've heard that "some people never grow up—
they just grow old." Most of us addicts (me, too)
were rebellious and defiant as children, and just
kept on keeping on with that attitude as we grew
older. I liked living on the edge. I was an outlaw
from the Establishment. The fast lane wasn't fast
enough. I lived for excitement, kicks, highs, but I
wasn't satisfied with just getting high; I wanted to
be *way* too high. "Live fast, die young, and leave a
beautiful corpse behind" was my motto. I didn't
like authority figures—the cops, my teachers, my
parents, or anyone else who tried to influence my
behavior.

In recovery, I've learned that my rebellious
attitude and behavior is a sign of immaturity. I've
become aware that my defiance and grandiosity
have no place in recovery. Now I cooperate with
life. I don't want to be an outlaw any more.

17. 12 REWARDS TO THE 12 STEP PROGRAM

1.   Hope instead of desperation;
2.   Faith instead of despair;
3.   Courage instead of fear;

4.   Peace of mind instead of confusion;
5.   Self-respect instead of self-contempt;
6.   Self-confidence instead of helplessness;
7.   The respect of others instead of their pity
     and contempt;
8.   A clean conscience instead of a sense of
     guilt;
9.   Real friendships instead of loneliness;
10. A clean pattern of life instead of a pur-
     poseless existence;
11. The love and understanding of our fami-
     lies instead of their doubts and fears;
12. The freedom of a happy life instead of the
     bondage of an addiction.

18.   IT BECOMES A HABIT

I could handle things myself,
And that became a habit.
I didn't face my problems,
And that became a habit.
I began to drink on a daily basis,
And that became a habit.
I started to be the problem of my family,
And that became a habit.
I started to procrastinate,
And that became a habit.

Except to bargain, I rarely prayed,
And that became a habit.
I became sick, guilty, and hopeless,
And that became a habit.
I came to meetings,
And that became a habit.
I didn't drink one day at a time,
And that became a habit.
I started to work the Program,
And that became a habit.
I started to pray,
And that became a habit.
I began to have hope and gratitude,
And that became a habit.
I started to love you, my family, and myself,
And that became a habit.
Thank God we can change our habits. H.O.W.?
Honesty, **O**penmindedness, **W**illingness,
"One Day at a Time."

19. THE SAME OLD CHOICES

When I got up this morning I was faced with
the same choice that I face every day of my life.

Is the day going to be a **bore** and a **chore** or
will it be an **adventure**?

Needless to say, in my life, I haven't always made the right choice at that moment, and in the world of reality there are tragedies and events beyond our control.

But I believe that with the tools the Program has given me I do have a choice.

In fact, if I truly start my day by asking for my Higher Power's protection and care with complete abandon and then just go on and be myself then I have a right to **expect** the day to be an adventure, and you know what—it happens.

At times in my life I have allowed others to make that choice for me. When I was using there was no possibility of choice. So, I am forced to accept the one fact that I ran from all of my life—I am **responsible**.

Even God cannot make that choice for me. Granted it is helpful to be surrounded by good friends and loved ones, but it is not **required**. I have learned to have a great day alone with God if I so choose.

I love the Third Step prayer which says, "relieve me of the bondage of self." I usually learn things the hard way, and today I know by my own long and painful experience that it really is **that simple**.

20. NO MORE FUN

The day was Friday the 13th, and I found myself in a treatment center. My first thought was, "It's true about Friday the 13th. This is the most unlucky day of my life." My second thought was, "This is it, no more fun."

It took about a week for the haze to lift, and for me to come to the realization that what I had been doing was *not* fun. I could only recall the first half-hour after I started using and the next morning I would fight the inevitable hangover with another drink. What used to work a magic spell for me in the past turned into a private hell. I never went out much anymore, and when I did I painfully paced my drinking until I could get home and drink the way I really wanted. I was frightened of people, places, and things, and so I isolated myself. No, I wasn't having a lot of fun anymore.

For the first year of sobriety I wasn't in pursuit of fun. I was busy going to meetings, reading the Big Book, and working the steps to the best of my ability. Slowly I started to appreciate flowers, sunsets, and the taste of a good meal.

The odd thing is I didn't go in search of fun, but I did discover joy. Joy is something I didn't know about before, and it is a more satisfying and lasting feeling. For me, joy is a by-product of recovery, meetings, working the steps, being willing to change, and being grateful to my Higher Power.

Oh, yes, you have probably guessed. I now consider Friday the 13th the luckiest day of my life.

21. LETTING GO

To let go doesn't mean to stop caring; it means I can't do it for someone else.

To let go is not to cut myself off; it is the realization that I can't control another.

To let go is not to enable, but to allow learning from natural consequences.

To let go is to admit powerlessness, which means the outcome is not in my hands.

To let go is not to try to change or blame another; I can only change myself.

To let go is not to care for, but to care about.

To let go is not to fix, but to be supportive.

To let go is not to judge, but to allow another to be a human being.

To let go is not to be in the middle arranging outcomes, but to allow others to effect their own outcomes.

To let go is not to be protective; it is to permit another to face reality.

To let go is not to deny, but to accept.

To let go is not to nag, scold, or argue, but to search out my own shortcomings and to correct them.

To let go is not to adjust everything to my desires, but to take each day as it comes and to cherish the moment.

To let go is not to criticize and regulate anyone, but to try to become what I dream I can be.

To let go is not to regret the past, but to grow and live for the future.

To let go is to fear less and love more.

22. PARENTS

I'd like to share with you how I got reacquainted with my Higher Power. But to do so, I'll share an experience I had, early in my recovery, with my parents.

As a result of my addiction, my relationship with my parents had sunk to the point that there was absolutely **nothing** between us but contempt, hurt, hate, pain, distress, and anger.

We were completely void of any love for one another. All we had was the innate feeling, between parents and child—that "I love you because we're related, but I hate what you've become" sort of love.

Upon joining the Program and taking my own inventory, I realized I had made many mistakes regarding my relationship with my parents and had to "set things right" as soon as I was able.

Now, this didn't come easy for me nor did it come all at once. I began with the basics: be nice, change my attitude toward them, accept them as they were.

Then I started to do little things: smile, help clean the house, do a load of laundry. You know . . . nice, simple, positive things.

As I did this, I began to feel better and they began to respond in kind. Slowly, as I worked on our relationship, it began to get easier. Today, my parents and I have a beautiful, loving, caring relationship. *What a miracle!*

When I think about this, I see that this is exactly how I developed a relationship with my Higher Power. I began simply by accepting Him and doing little things. Things like praying in the morning and evening—seeking His guidance for me. And guess what? The results were the same. I began to feel better, and my relationship with my Higher Power bloomed into a beautiful, loving, growing thing.

So can we all, if we start with willingness, acceptance, and the simple things.

23. MATURITY

Maturity is the growing awareness that you are neither wonderful nor hopeless.

It has been said to be the making of a place between what is and what might be. It isn't a destination. It's a journey. It is the moment when you wake up after some grief, or staggering blow, and find that you're going to live after all!

It is the moment when you find out that something you have long believed in isn't so, and parting with the old idea, find that you're still you; the moment you discover somebody can do your job as well as you can and you go on doing it anyway; the moment you realize you are forever alone, but so is everybody else, and so in some way you are more together than ever; and a hundred other moments when you find out who you are.

It is letting life happen in its own good order and making the most of what there is.

24. RISKING—A GIFT OF THE PROGRAM

I've always been a very fearful person. Alcohol was my "liquid courage." As a young child, summer camp was out of the question. Being away from home, even overnight, was frightening. Making friends as a teenager seemed an impossible task. The kids seemed to be in groups and I just could not figure out how to be a part. At age 13, I had a "date" and almost passed out with fear when he held my hand. Does this sound wimpy and immature? Perhaps. But the world always looked so big to me, and I always felt so small.

Discovering the wonders of alcohol at age 15 turned all this around. Not only did I feel courageous when I drank, I had the sense that I could outdo anyone at anything. Vacations now meant going to the river—drinking, water skiing, drinking some more. Making friends became easy. Bad John, Dirty Ray, and I got along just fine. Boyfriends? I had lots of them. Perhaps I don't remember their names and would prefer not to remember the way I acted in their company, but I did have a full dance card—and I wasn't wimpy any more. I was full of courage, confidence, and alcohol.

It was in 1980 that I had my last drink at the age of 18. With that final glass of wine went my inner strength. I was filled with fear again when I entered the doors of Alcoholics Anonymous. I stayed that way for a long time. Risking friendships, travel, dating, job challenges seemed overwhelming. You (the members of AA) seemed to know how to live and to be comfortable without drinking. I wanted what you had. I still do! I followed your directions. I came to meetings. I worked the Steps. And I didn't drink, no matter what.

The reason I keep doing these things is directly due to the results I've gotten from your example. In the past eight years, I've traveled the U.S., Canada, and seven countries throughout the world—by myself! I've run the marathon and competed in two triathlons. I've made many interesting friends and it's hard to remember the lonely days. Men? My dance card is full once again, but this time with a difference. I feel a self-respect and dignity that I've never known. I even remember names today. There are many experiences I've had and will continue to have because of you and the Program.

Not only do I thank you for my life . . . I sincerely thank you for the **quality** of my life.

25. FORGIVE ME!

I have had some real difficulty with forgiveness. Don't misunderstand me. It hasn't been hard to forgive **them**. My problem has been in forgiving me.

Intellectually, I know my addiction is a disease, but a little voice keeps telling me that "I should have known better. I wasn't raised to do the things I did."

I had high moral values and ended up doing all the things I hated—lying, cheating, stealing, being phony and a hypocrite. I came from a family of prudes and became promiscuous. I was taught to be responsible, and became irresponsible. I could go on and on.

I find it hard to swallow that "everything I did, I thought was a good idea at the time," although I know it's true. (The first time I heard that in a meeting, I wanted to puke.)

I have been going to retreats for the past few years and the first couple of times, I was absolutely miserable. I'm happy to say, it is getting better.

Last year, the retreat master sent us out for 30 minutes or more of silent meditation. I went to our air-conditioned room, opened a Pepsi, and lit a cigarette. Suddenly I was overcome by the feeling that I could not meditate in comfort. I proceeded to go outside in the blazing sun, sit on the hard cement, without Pepsi or cigarettes, and promptly went nuts.

This year I was able to sit outside in a semi-comfortable chair with my Pepsi and cigarettes, and you know, instead of smoking, I watched the birds and marveled at nature. Maybe there is hope for me yet.

I was never able to understand my earlier reaction, but believe today that I was still hanging on to the idea that I was a "bad" person and not a "sick person." I feel unworthy of God's love and keep thinking His love and grace must be earned.

I have been told time and time again that I am worthy. My trouble has been in believing it.

If there is anyone else out there having these feelings, all I can say is that it takes time and I do have many moments when I feel that I am worthwhile. Maybe someday I will accept the fact that I cannot change the past, but can be deserving of a good future—by the grace of God.

I must remember that I am a "sick person trying to get well" and not a "bad person trying to get good."

I must learn to forgive me.

26. THE GOD WORD

My lifesaver, upon entering the program, was the idea that I could have a God, *as I understood Him*. The only problem with that idea was that the word God would cause me to relate with the God of my early religious training, not my understanding. That, in turn, would not have given me a spiritual foundation, which would have denied me this wonderful program and way of life.

Therefore, I began calling Him "The Man Upstairs." This played with my head, too, for I felt it might be disrespectful. I finally asked a friend, who calls his God "Big Leroy." His answer was that no matter how you addressed Him it was okay, as He knew to whom you were talking. Since then I have heard "Higher Power," "HP," "The Guy in the Sky," and hosts of other phrases.

You will note that all of the above are harder to pronounce than just "God." Being somewhat lazy, I now have no problem with the term "God."

To have denied myself this spiritual program due to a hangup over a name would have been a waste.

Call Him or Her anything you wish, just call. Like all aspects of our Program, it's simple. God is just a one-syllable word!

27. GIVING UP, CLEANING UP, MAKING UP, AND GROWING UP

Growing up is something I'm trying to do, because that's part of the 12 Steps—giving up, cleaning up, making up, and growing up—all such fun things to do, right? But so far, trying to live the 12 Steps of our Program has kept me clean and sober for four years. Even though I'm not sure I want to grow up, I *am* sure I don't ever want to relapse.

Learning, change, and pain are all things associated in my mind with growing up. But I also think growing up has something to do with living life on life's terms, knowing when to turn loose my will and go with my Higher Power's will, being responsible for my actions and owning the results of those actions. I think it's being able to put into practice "to thine own self be true" while detracting as little as possible from the well-being of others.

In other words, it's practicing the principles of the Program in all my affairs. I've been told no one ever graduates during recovery. I don't plan on ever finishing growing up. It's a process. I'm more grown up now than I was three years ago when I started recovery, and I hope to be able to say the same thing three years from now.

28. YOUNG OR OLD, IT'S ALL THE SAME

I celebrated my twenty-second birthday in a treatment center. By the time I walked into these rooms, I was drinking a fifth a day, every day. My coke habit was out of control. I had been fired from three jobs, been raped, physically abused by a "boyfriend," totalled my car, and was arrested with a .25 alcohol content. The pain I was feeling was nothing compared to the pain I was causing my family and loved ones. I had no self-respect or self-esteem left. I had just enough life left in me to get me through those treatment center doors.

When I began my adventure into 12 Step recovery, I heard many stories—some were of men who had been drinkers for 40 years. Other stories were of the "housewife" alcoholics with 20 years of sobriety who were drinking when "treatment" wasn't an option. There were stories from husbands and wives, doctors and lawyers, landscapers and construction workers, students and teachers, bus drivers and mail men. They were short, tall, fat, thin, black, white, young, old.

I heard the story of a 14-year-old girl who was involved in gangs, an alcoholic and drug addict with thoughts of suicide. I listened to a 17-year-old boy who had five felony counts against him, no place to live, and wanted help for his addictions. I heard the story of a 16-year-old boy who wanted serenity and this 12 Step Program, but his **father** was still using and promised to buy him a car if he came home and got high with dad.

All those stories made me realize that this wonderful world of recovery and the Fellowship of A.A., C.A., N.A. is for everyone and anyone, regardless of sex, race, religion, or AGE. The pain and suffering is the same whether you're 14 or 40, whether you drank or used for a few years or 50. Everyone's story is unique, but we share our recovery together.

29. RESENTMENT AND UNCONDITIONAL LOVE

By the time I got to the Program, I had lost all self-respect and self-esteem. There were no boundaries, no guidelines. My life was insane. I didn't have the guts to kill myself. I had chosen a slow death through my addiction.

My addiction had led me to a relationship that was very abusive, both physically and emotionally. This man promised me the world and said he'd take care of me. All I got was a few rides in an ambulance and a lot of visits to the emergency room. But at least these events sped up my decision to get help.

Three weeks into treatment, I was told I was pregnant. After a lot of discussion and prayers, I decided to keep the baby. Three months later, I miscarried. This was very hard for me to accept at first. I had heard so much talk of "unconditional love." This was something I knew the baby could give me; something I had never known.

Eventually, I found that unconditional love— through family and the fellowship of sober friends. Today, I can accept that losing the baby was God's will and that there was a reason for it. I have realized that, with only a couple of months in recovery, I wasn't able to love myself, let alone a newborn baby.

For several months, I accepted that unconditional love from others in the Program. I let them "love me until I was able to love myself." Today, I can look in the mirror and actually like what I see. An act as simple as that was something I couldn't do before. Every now and then, while I'm looking in the mirror, I say out loud, "I love you." Try it— it works if you work it; it won't if you don't!

30. RELATIONSHIPS

We all probably believe our recovery Program will give us new chances to form relationships. This may be frightening to us, because our experience with intimate friendships has been pretty rocky. They've been a source of much pain and misery for many of us. We have only to look around to see that for most people relationships are not easy.

When we work our Steps, we discover how much shame, guilt, pity, and anger we had for ourselves and our partners. We had invested enormous amounts of time, energy, and personal resources in those relationships. The Program has revealed a need to completely overhaul our attitudes about intimate and personal relationships.

The Program helps me be a better partner in a relationship. Most of the time I never really needed better partners. I just needed to be a better person.

31. DESIRE

The words "alcoholic" and "addict" are heard often in recovery. What does it take to become one of these? When do you know? For some of us it takes years, losing cars, houses, jobs, family, and loved ones. For others, it is simply waking up with one too many hangovers or after one too many runs. It seems to be that tough, or even that easy.

I am an addict. For me it was tough. The one thing I have learned in my recovery is that you don't **have** to say you're an "alcoholic" or an "addict" to begin the Program. You just have to have the "desire" to quit using. All the other stuff really doesn't matter.

No matter how different we all are, how old or young we are, what we drank, or what drug we did or didn't use, there is room in the Program for those who honestly and truthfully have the desire to stop using. It only takes a desire to change your life for the better and a willingness to quit using mind-altering substances, just for today.

32. MEETINGS

We are told that every meeting we attend will be a good meeting. It takes the good and bad meeting—the good and bad speaker—to make the Program work. Our sponsor will tell us there are no bad meetings; all meetings are good, some are just better than others. Newcomers are asked not to even consider whether the meetings are good or bad. "Just bring your body and the mind will follow," and "take what you need and leave the rest."

Even when we think we didn't get much out of a meeting, we will find that many others who were there benefited a great deal. We may remember something we heard at a "bad" meeting more often than what we heard at a "good" meeting. The old-timers tell us, "The most important part of any meeting, for you, is the moment you walk through the door into it. It's not so much what you do there, it's the fact that you are there."

We need to remember some meetings may be better than others, but it's more important that we're there.

33. EMOTIONS

As we start our journey down the road of recovery, we find we experience many feelings that we weren't aware of when we were using. It's not that these feelings are good or bad. It's what we do with them. Sometimes we "think" or "feel like" we're bad people. All the good and bad feelings are helping us grow, spiritually and emotionally. We learn it's okay to laugh and smile. It's even okay to cry. When feelings surface, we step back, slow down, and really take a look at how we're feeling and what's causing it. Maybe we do a spot check inventory.

A lot of times we find these negative emotions are caused by our own doing, even though we think something or someone else is at fault. We realize we don't have to act on them. We can call a fellow member or our sponsor, and work through it. By working the Twelve Steps in our everyday lives, we can accept ourselves and other people as they are more easily, and ask others to accept us as we are. Acceptance makes our feelings easier to deal with.

34. PAST MISTAKES

They say around the Program, "if you turn it over and don't let go of it, you'll be upside down."

A lot of unhappiness comes from dwelling on past mistakes and failures. Our Higher Power can do many things for us: remove a lifelong compulsion to drink, to drug, to overeat, to gamble; remove all kinds of character defects such as lying, cheating, stealing, adultery. Our Higher Power can help us with many things, but our HP cannot force us to accept our past. If we choose to walk around with shame and guilt about the past, that's our choice.

It has been the collective wisdom of our Fellowship that many people have relapsed because they couldn't let go and accept their past mistakes. We all, each one of us, were born imperfect. It is not surprising that this imperfection, along with our addiction, has caused us trouble along the way. We learn how to live with our past mistakes by practicing and using the tools of the Program.

35. RESENTMENT AND MY HIGHER POWER

When I first heard the word "resentment" and slowly began to understand its meaning, it seemed too much to deal with. And boy, was it! When I came into this Program, I "resented" everyone, including God. During all the years of using drugs and alcohol, it was always "Why me?" Why was I being punished? Every job I lost, every relationship destroyed, every car wrecked, was always someone else's fault, never my own.

Once I really started working the Program and began helping others, I began to realize I had a trail of resentments which kept leading me around and around in circles. I was stuck, and wasn't able to get back on the path to my recovery. I would turn it over to my Higher Power, and within a day or two, I was taking it right back. But I kept asking for guidance and strength from my Higher Power, and one day I woke up and the resentments and the anger were gone. I realized I had finally put a detour in that trail of resentments. At last my belief and commitment to my Higher Power paid off. That has made my commitment to my recovery stronger.

36. CAME TO BELIEVE

When we surrendered to our Higher Power, the journey began. Many of us had trouble believing that a God existed when we began our recovery program, because for years we thought we were the master of our own affairs. We paid attention to no desires or wishes but our own.

When we realized how much help we needed, we first looked to other members and our group for support. By rejecting at first the idea of a Power *higher* than ourselves, many of us did accept the idea of a Power *other* than ourselves. As we have made spiritual progress, most of us now have a clear and ongoing belief in a Higher Power that we choose to call God.

It's important to our recovery to rely on our Higher Power, as our own belief in a Higher Power is what can and does save us from our addiction. Only two of the Steps talk about addiction. The other ten talk about spiritual growth. We have a firm foundation for spiritual health and spiritual progress when we continue to believe in our Higher Power.

37. KEEP IT SIMPLE

In our days, weeks, months, and years of recovery, each day will bring us people or circumstances with which we may try to complicate our lives and our progress. This is when we ask for "the serenity to accept the things we cannot change, courage to change the things we can, and the wisdom to know the difference." We do this by trusting in a Power greater than ourselves and by applying the simple Twelve Step Program. Keeping it simple will help simplify the demands of any situation.

38. WORKING THROUGH DEPRESSION

It took a while to adjust from the physical withdrawal of my addiction. When I began to feel better physically, my emotions and thinking caught up with what was happening. Wow! Was I depressed! All I could do was think about my past and feel anger, resentment, and fear. Was that what recovery was, going from the *fast* lane to the *past* lane? The pain was too much. And what about this gigantic chip on my shoulder?

I was very close to relapse, or to actually putting into action my thoughts of suicide. There was no single magical event that brought me out of and through this terrible time in early recovery. I learned in treatment how important it was to ask for help, but I took my time before I did it!

I owe a great deal to my sponsor. She got me to start working through my pain and to begin to see the healing available in working the 12 Steps. My life had been one of being split off from myself. Most of my character defects were learned as a child in order to cope and survive.

I could probably write a book on what happened to me before recovery and after, but I'll just give you some of the highlights of what I've learned.

Maybe I never really had much of a chance to lead a "normal" life. Things were done to me that shouldn't happen to anyone, ever. The Steps have led me out of focusing on those awful negative events to focusing on what I can do, with the help of my friends and my Higher Power.

I've been able to forgive others and myself, to acknowledge and accept what I can do today. When I based my outlook and moods on the bad things in the past, I went nowhere. I denied myself the possibility of a better today, a better tomorrow.

I won't tell you that just thinking positive thoughts is the way to get away from self-pity, self-blame, and self-hatred, but it is part of it. First, I had to want out, then I had to get help, and finally, I had to get to work, with the awareness I had to *act* my way out instead of *thinking* my way out. I had to go through the pain, not around it.

I *can* tell you that a whole load of pain has gone away by itself, by my staying with the Program, staying willing to do the work, and exerting the effort to help myself.

39. AMENDS

I am a 25-year-old female. I celebrated my eighteenth birthday in a treatment center for alcohol and drug abuse. I have been sober ever since. When I walked through those doors and entered into the Program, I had burnt all bridges behind me. I had been kicked out of my mother's and grandma's house. My father had evicted me from one of his apartments. I had borrowed hundreds of dollars from a friend of mine and never paid her back. I was asked to be the maid of honor at my best friend's wedding and didn't show up. I was engaged to be married and told him to get out of my life. These are just a few examples of the things I had done.

It took me a long time to get over the guilt of all the pain I had caused to the people who supported me and loved me the most. I guess that's how it always is.

I immediately tried to make amends for my wrongs, but I realized it took more than just saying "I'm sorry." Talk's cheap, and I had done a lot of it when I was using.

There is no way I can ever pay back the money my parents spent on me. There is no way I can take back the pain I caused. All they ask of me is to stay sober. That's amends enough for them. My parents tell me every day how nice it is to have their daughter back.

Some of my friends have accepted my amends; some have not (most of these are still using). This is something I must learn to accept. The only thing I can do is make the effort to mend the relationship. The decision is then left up to the other person to accept or reject my efforts. I ask my Higher Power for strength to accept them the way they are, and pray that they can do the same.

40. CHOICE

I'm often asked "how" I stay sober. For me, it's simple. Drinking and drugging isn't an option in my life any more.

At the age of twenty-one, I came into the Program totally burnt out. In my eyes, I had used up all my options. The only choices left were death or sobriety. I chose sobriety.

There were still a couple of YETs that I did avoid, but for me, my problems and the pain I was feeling were more than enough for me to begin.

41. CHARACTER DEFECTS

Working the Program comes easier for some and more difficult for others. There comes a time in recovery where we all take our inventory, a time when we must become honest with ourselves and really take notice of those "character defects." Remaining abstinent from chemical mood changers can be easy. It's dealing with yourself and life on life's terms that becomes more difficult once the booze and drugs are out of the picture.

Personal change can happen quickly, but usually works best if we go slow, "one day at a time." If we try to change too quickly, we can get discouraged. Think of all the time we spent acquiring those "defects of character" while we were using. It may take just as long and sometimes longer to correct them. We may find ourselves wanting to cry all the time. We may feel as if there's something missing in our lives and in the Program. We may be critical of others too often. We may not feel like going to meetings any more.

These are usually clues that it's time to get honest with ourselves. As painful as it may be, we need to begin the work.

42. 13TH STEP

I am a young female member, and I have been in the Fellowship for a little over a year now. I've been sad and lonely since I stopped using and have been trying to overcome my feelings in my early stages of growing up; I'm still a little mixed up. And I have some extra problems with which to cope.

First, I've had a few of the male members trying to get me to have sex with them; and although one or two realize how much that has disturbed me, they don't seem capable of understanding that when I say no, I mean NO. They don't seem to understand, or care, that I have a very good reason for saying no. I just do not want to have sex with them.

It's not that I'm anti-men; it's just that I've changed a lot since I came into these rooms. I've been trying so hard to make a decent life for myself and not "sleep around" any more. Before I came to the Program, I had been used and abused and hurt far too often; now I'm struggling to stay abstinent, and that is difficult enough without having to cope with male members pestering me to get at my body. It not only stops my progress; it increases my fear and anger, two things I have to get rid of or I will go back out and start screwing up my life again.

Another difficulty is trying to cope with disappointment. On one particular occasion, after successfully resisting repeated efforts to get at my body, we parted on good terms. I am basically a friendly, loving person, and perhaps a little naive. I phoned him the next day to make sure we were still going to a meeting (we had made plans before the previous day), and he assured me we would still go. But he didn't turn up for me. I felt so let down.

As if all this were not enough, one member has been scheming more than the others, trying to seduce me away from my better way of life that I'm gradually building with the help of the Program and two caring sponsors. This man has been talking to me in a sly way, trying to get me to reveal intimate details of my past. But what really frightened me was when he told me that alcohol would not affect me now!

Fortunately for me, I'm not that stupid. I know very well what booze will do, and I want none of it. I want to stay away from alcohol and get well and live a sober life.

If these people want to get sober and not stay one of the "un-drunks," I suggest they start examining themselves. They may need help to solve their problems, but help is available if they seek it.

But what about me? How can I make progress and get a little serenity? All this reminds me of the 13th Step I read about in *Easy Does It*, my daily meditation book:

"The 13th Step is taken by members who suffer from the delusion that sex can cure their addiction.

Both women and men practice the selfish 13th Step. They're not always easy to spot. Some go to meetings and appear to work the Program, while others just sit around clubhouses, eyeballing members of the opposite sex (always newcomers), waiting for their chance to pounce. Newcomers, being somewhat bewildered, sometimes confuse lust with love and fall victim to this dangerous game.

Many newcomers have run from the Program when they realize the 'help' being offered was a mask for sexual favors. Many of these unsuspecting newcomers never come back. Sex has never cured anyone's obsessions or addictions.

I am responsible for not using my experience in the Program to take advantage of a fellow member, especially a newcomer. If I see anyone 13th Stepping, I will do what I can to tell the person how unlucky the 13th Step is."

43. MY GANG OR OUR FELLOWSHIP

My life has been spent in housing projects throughout the city. Dad split just after I was born, and I don't know where he is now. My oldest brother is in and out of prison—you name it, he's done it. My sister has two kids and works the streets to support her habit. Mom did what she could, but most of her time is spent on finding her next fix.

I got kicked out of school when I was 13 for selling crack and being involved in a local gang. I joined the gang because they gave me the attention and love I couldn't get at home. They took care of me. Once I got kicked out of school, I realized that was "cool"—more time for the "the gang" and more time to sell dope and most of all, more time to get high. I was busted by the cops a lot, but I was just a kid, so I knew they couldn't do anything. Mom was never around. My sister would usually come pick me up when I got busted—that is, when I could find her. The city tried to put me in foster homes but that didn't work either. I was having the time of my life, so I thought!

One day, I was sitting at a bus stop waiting to go somewhere. I didn't even know where I wanted to go. I'd been high on crack for three days. I hadn't eaten or bathed in days. I had no money. I didn't even know if I had a home to go home to. After a few minutes, I noticed this older guy sitting next to me. He asked if he could help. Of course I told him to shut up and mind his own business. Little did I know this man would be the one to save my life.

The next thing I knew, I was sitting in the basement of some church at an NA meeting, listening to people from the same neighborhood, with the same problems I had. I've kept coming back ever since. Today I call that man at the bus stop "my sponsor."

My recovery is contagious. Mom is waiting for a bed in a treatment center, and is going to meetings in the meantime. My sister is off the streets and home with her kids. My brother—well, he's still in prison, but he's next!

Today I realize just how sick I really was. I'm working on getting my G.E.D. and I've found the love and attention I thought I was getting from the gang through the Program. And **this** love is unconditional.

44. DATING

I was quite shocked in early recovery to realize I didn't know the first thing about dating. I had gone out with a lot of young women when I was using. As long as I had coke, I was remarkably popular. To ask someone out, I just asked if she would like to do some coke. Getting a date was easy, and they all said I was the best, and they all said they loved me (as long as the coke lasted).

I didn't think much about dating in early recovery. I was just hanging on and going to a lot of meetings. The thought of someone going out with me just because I was me was confusing. Why would anyone want to go with me without some "hook," money or drugs?

My sponsor suggested I first learn how to be friends with women before I began dating. It took awhile to get my head on straight about this area of my recovery. Recovery means more than just stopping drugs. It has to do with every aspect of the way you treat yourself and others.

45. SINGLE AND SEXY

There is a problem not often discussed around the meeting rooms. Nevertheless, it is a problem.

When we were loaded, we sometimes lacked morality. The old Country & Western song, "All the Girls Get Prettier at Closing Time" was a fact. With alcohol or drugs removing our inhibitions, it was easy to become involved in affairs or relationships.

Today, we are clean and sober. There are many divorced people in the Program as a result of their addiction. And like myself, there is also an influx of young, single people coming to the Program due to an acute awareness of chemical dependency.

We are physically, morally, and spiritually bankrupt when we come to the Program. It is necessary to remove the guilt feelings of the past by *"Admit[ting] to God, to ourselves, and to another human being, the exact nature of our wrongs."*

We must then continue to take a personal inventory and improve our conscious contact with God as we understand Him. Only then, *well past our first year of recovery,* may we hope to make any major changes in our lives. We must always remember that our primary purpose is to stay abstinent. Only when we work the Program are we useful.

By working the Steps of the Program and adhering to the principles, we find ourselves getting better. Feelings and emotions begin to return. An honest look within ourselves finds sexual yearning again rising.

A dilemma arises. What should one do? Most meetings are mixed and many friendly relationships can occur. A love and trust is built up between two people in the Program. To destroy this trust can be catastrophic to either or both parties. A relapse could be in the making.

The answers don't come easy. Individually, we have to decide for ourselves what we must do. The easiest, softest way I've heard is to go get wasted and pick up one of those people at closing time. But this is *not* the answer. On the other hand, there is difficulty involved with complete celibacy, although this works for some. For most of us, who realize that we are not saints, we stand at a turning point.

Because it is a personal decision, we find that going back to the "Four Absolutes" which helped the early members of my Fellowship could give us a guide. Enter the relationship with complete *honesty*. Desires and motives must be absolutely *unselfish*. We must decide if our *love* is emotional or physical. If it is physical, forget it. The *purity* of our intentions must be examined. These decisions must be made with guidance from our Higher Power.

There is no pat answer. Serious consideration should be given to any relationship. The wrong decision can affect not only ourselves, but our friends and our group. The Absolutes can be extremely helpful when we want to do the right thing and the answer is not obvious.

When our recovery has a foundation firm enough to withstand stress, then we are ready to live, and love, in God's light. We are reminded in the Program that "Our sex powers were God-given and therefore good, neither to be used lightly or selfishly nor to be despised and loathed."

What comes from our Higher Power is to be honored and treated with respect. Our sexuality has unlimited potential for good. We have so often turned this power in on ourselves and been destroyed by it, or allowed it to destroy others.

The Steps let us change our feelings about sex so that these new feelings can encourage wholesome relationships. When we walk with our Higher Power, our self-will doesn't run riot over our sex lives. Our spiritual awakening washes over all our relationships, even our most tender and personal.

We gain a new sense of respect. We learn we can love deeply. We find that sexuality is a powerful, life-giving force that enriches, bonds, and commits us to a special person. We no longer have to face remorse and guilt from uncontrolled desires.

May I rediscover the joy in my God-given sexuality by treating myself and others with honor and respect.

46. RICH GIRL

Big house, designer clothes, and fancy cars. The rich girl—that's how people knew me.

My dad was always out of town on business. Mom kept busy with her shrink and her Valium. That left me to do whatever I wanted. I chose to drink and drug, trying to make all my problems go away. My grades started falling from "A"s to "C"s and "D"s, but no one noticed. I wrecked three different cars, and still no one noticed. Dad's excuse for everything was that I needed a vacation, so he'd send me off somewhere for a week or two and give me another car.

The further I got into my addiction, the further I slid into deep depression. All I wanted was an easy way out, someone to make the pain go away. I felt I had nowhere to turn, no place to run. That's when thoughts of suicide started entering my mind. I thought that would be an "easy way out." All the hurting would stop. It would bring an end to the insanity. I'd show **them!**

I tried first with my Mom's pills. Then I tried slitting my wrists. I made four different attempts, none of them successful. The thoughts of suicide became a new addiction. I was convinced I wanted to die. The last attempt was the closet to being successful. At that time my mother and father gave me their last gift—28 days at a treatment center.

My first reaction was immediate anger. I didn't need treatment! It was all the "other" people, places, and things that ruined my life, not the alcohol and drugs.

My first two weeks I went along with it and told everyone what they wanted to hear. Then I heard the story of a girl who had left treatment and gone "back out" and used. She didn't make it back. She took her own life. That story was my turning point and the first step to my recovery.

Along with some counseling, group discussions, and the Fellowship, today I'm living a new life. I'm not known as the "rich girl" any more. I live a much simpler life and am self-supporting, and I do it all clean and sober.

47. RELAPSE

It seems you hear the word "relapse" often around the Program. It's said in several different ways, but it always means the same thing. Someone has gone back out for more!

For some, this is necessary. Some people think they don't have a problem. That's called "denial." Others think they can control their addiction. They forget the First Step. Then there are the ones who just haven't had enough. Some of them make it back. A lot of them don't.

There are some cases where "relapse" becomes a part of recovery. It's not suggested, but it's also not the end of the world. That's the wonderful part of this Program. No matter how many times it takes, you're always welcomed back.

The question often arises in the Program as to why "so and so" relapsed after time in recovery. The answer is *dishonesty*. Most of us agree that before we came into the Program, we hid behind a mask and didn't let anyone really know us. Since coming into the Program, some of us hide behind the dreaded "Recovery Mask."

When someone is wearing a Recovery Mask, they deceive others into believing that they're doing well in recovery. The real danger lies in deceiving themselves into believing the same thing. One thing this false image can't live with is truth. It would be helpful for them to ask themselves, "When was the last time I shared what was really going on inside me, in my innermost world, with a close friend, my sponsor, or my home group?"

It does me harm to hide behind a recovery mask. If I do, I may relapse because I'm not sharing my experience, strength, and hope, but only my opinions, attitudes and advice.

48. DOING IT FOR MYSELF

I had been in the program three months when I had a relapse. As I look back on it now, it's easy to explain what happened. I had stopped using and joined the Program just to get my parents off my back.

It was easy to go back out and find drugs to do. I knew exactly where to go. The day after my relapse I was overwhelmed by guilt and very disappointed with myself. Somehow I got the courage to go back to my group and tell them about my relapse. I'm glad I didn't stay out there on a long, destructive relapse before I went back. My group told me I hadn't lost everything; I had just made a mistake, nothing more and nothing less.

I look back now, two clean years later, and think of my relapse as an educational experience.

It's an experience that's not necessary for most people to get the Program, but I started to listen and work the program when I went back. I began to change my behavior and attitudes so further detours wouldn't happen. But this time I'm doing it for myself, not for anyone else.

49. THANK YOU, HP

Thank you, my Higher Power, for Life . . . a life with meaning in which I can be me, a life of courage to replace the fear. It feels so good to be young and alive, to carry my head high and to keep my mind clear so that I can see and enjoy the truly beautiful world in which You have placed me! Please don't ever let me take my life for granted.

Thank you, my Higher Power, for Love . . . for helping me to sow love where only hatred could grow before, for helping me to love and understand my parents, and for showing me that, no matter what they do, they still love me. It is wonderful to know what friendship really is—to have that sense of hope which assures me that I don't have to be lonely any more.

Thank you, my Higher Power, for Joy . . . the kind of joy that wells within me when I know that my life is in the hands of One Who understands and cares as no other can, a joy that brings with it a beautiful feeling of inner peace.

And thank you, most of all, Higher Power, for being the greatest friend a young person like me can have.

50. JUST FOR TODAY

Just for today I will try to live through this day only, and not tackle my whole life problem at once. I can do something for twelve hours that would appall me if I felt that I had to keep it up for a lifetime.

Just for today I will be happy. This assumes to be true what Abraham Lincoln said, that "Most folks are as happy as they make up their minds to be."

Just for today I will adjust myself to what is, and not try to adjust everything else to my own desires, I will take my "luck" as it comes, and fit myself to it.

Just for today I will try to strengthen my mind, I will study, I will learn something useful, I will not be a mental loafer, I will read something that requires effort, thought and concentration.

Just for today I will exercise my soul in three ways: I will do somebody a good turn, and not get found out; if anybody knows of it, it will not count. I will do at least two things I don't want to do—just for exercise. I will not show anyone that my feelings are hurt; they may be hurt, but today I will not show it.

Just for today I will be agreeable. I will look as well as I can, dress becomingly, talk low, act courteously, criticize not one bit, not find fault with anything, and not try to improve or regulate anybody except myself.

Just for today I will have a program. I may not follow it exactly, but I will have it. I will save myself from two pests: hurry and indecision.

Just for today I will have a quiet half hour all by myself, and relax. During this half hour, sometime, I will try to get a better perspective on my life.

Just for today I will be unafraid. I will enjoy that which is beautiful, and will believe that as I give to the world, so the world will give to me.

51. A HEALTHY DEPENDENCE

In my active addiction I confused love with dependence. My relationships suffered from my lack of emotional maturity. Manipulation seemed to be the key to my security, and I used people to achieve my selfish ends. People never seemed to live up to my demands, which left me feeling resentful toward everyone. When I hit bottom I found myself alone.

The grace of my Higher Power guided me to the Fellowship. I attended ninety meetings in ninety days, got a sponsor, began working the Twelve Steps, and didn't use. Slowly, I began to feel better. The Program was working for me and I wanted to share my recovery with others.

I wanted my parents to show their approval of my efforts. My anticipation of their approval proved to be unrealistic. They remained suspicious of my motives for several months. My dad said he was glad I wasn't using drugs, but added that he didn't think I had changed at all! My mom accused me of being loaded! I was hurt! Gradually, I learned that my recovery was not dependent on the approval of my parents.

I developed a more understanding attitude as a result of the Fourth Step. Manipulation was a tool I had used against my parents for many years. The lack of trust in our family would take time and effort to change. The Program taught me to take care of my recovery and leave my parents to my Higher Power. This philosophy has proved helpful in all my relationships.

I began dating my girlfriend from my using days. Now that I was clean things would work out for us, right? I took her to meetings with me and gave her literature to read. She was sick too, and I was going to help her.

I continued working the Program, but the relationship didn't seem to be working. She seemed resentful of my help. Why didn't she appreciate all I was doing to help her?

When I got honest, I could see my self-centered motives in the relationship. I wanted to help her to relieve my guilt. Thinking I was responsible for her problems created a desire in me to fix her. My sponsor reminded me that we are responsible for our own recovery. This does not mean I am responsible for the recovery of others. I had to let go of this relationship. I made amends for the harm I had caused and left the results to God. I pray for God's will to be done for her.

I lacked a feeling of self-worth. I was dependent on other people to provide positive feelings for me. This caused me to have unrealistic expectations for everyone and they always let me down. Then I would blame them for the way I felt. They were responsible for my problems, not me. Painful and valuable lessons were being learned, though I didn't know it at the time.

Recovery has taught me that I needed to accept responsibility for my problems and solutions. My feelings to a large extent are determined by my actions. When my actions are selfish, the results are negative feelings about myself and others. When I act in a kind and loving way, I am blessed with positive feelings. Check your feelings sometime after a Twelfth Step call or service work well done.

Recovery is teaching me to love myself in an unselfish way. I seek to relate in ways which encourage the well-being of others and myself. Though at times I make poor choices, recovery has given me the freedom to admit when I am wrong. I can learn from my mistakes, but if I don't learn the lesson from my experience, then I will have to experience the lesson again.

The Twelve Steps have been a process of spiritual growth. This has enabled me to feel the love of God. I am dependent on my Higher Power today. This type of dependence has been healthy for me. When my relationship with my Higher Power is right, I no longer depend on other people to live up to my demands. Then I have the freedom to give up control and live in true partnership with others.

Today I find the world a better place to live. It is easier to live in the world when I am not carrying it on my shoulders. My relationships are now a blessing rather than a burden. What a miracle to see my reflection in the eyes of others and like what I see!

52. HOPE AT AN EARLY AGE

Seven years ago today a desperate fifteen-year-old girl got loaded for the last time.

Willing to go any lengths after using for many years. Willing to listen to members say, "You're not an addict—you're too young. Come back after you've experienced some pain."

Remembering at age nine being used by adults just to stay high. Doing anything to get that next drug. Feeling desperate, alone, not even human. I remember thinking in my first few months in N.A., while relapsing—"why do I need to go through more pain? I want to get clean!"

With no one my age to relate to I just wish someone had explained the Third Tradition to me: "The only requirement for membership is the desire to stop using." There were some that looked into my eyes and saw the pain. They knew I had paid my dues. Putting all teasing aside—I surrendered to the Program. Being the youngest member of my area I struggled to be taken seriously. I had suffered enough. I learned that the Twelve Steps of Narcotics Anonymous can work just as well for me as they can for the addict who used for twenty-five years.

Today I'm twenty-two years old and have been clean for seven years. And in carrying the message of hope to young addicts, I am now the "old-timer" of my group. I'm respected and hope to change the attitude that age or the amount of time someone has used determines if N.A. is for them. If I had given in to this attitude I may not be alive today. The hell I lived in was so indescribable that the God-given Program of Narcotics Anonymous was my only hope.

There is hope! I have a choice. I never have to use again no matter how I feel, and that choice is available to all of us.

53. CHANGES

What a relief to allow others to be themselves. I then have time to work on me. This is a freedom the Program has given me.

I spent most of my life trying to change reality. People, places, and things were my problem (I thought). If only people would behave the way I wanted them everything would be okay. Of course people rarely cooperated, and I became frustrated and angry. I blamed them for my frustration and increased my efforts to change them. I became extremely confused, angry, and resentful. This only ended in more frustration. I was a victim, helpless against a hostile and sinful world. My only escape was the false sense of security I found in my active addiction.

When I became involved with the 12 Steps, I was beaten. I surrendered. I was taught that I could not change reality, but I could change my attitudes toward reality. A journal of my first year of recovery may have gone like this:

"There are so many things that need changing. Why do I always have to be the one to change? Go to meetings and don't pick up. Work the Steps. I hurt! It isn't worth it! Read. Talk to my sponsor. How can they laugh? I'm really hurting! Go to meetings and don't pick up. Work the Steps. One year in recovery. I have worked so hard— is this all I get? Keep going to meetings. People are beginning to change. I begin to laugh with them. I begin to laugh at myself. I'm getting better. I cry. What a relief!"

My recovery continues to progress with occasional lapses in my spiritual program. When I focus on my recovery, the world seems to be okay. I need to accept that I am always responsible for my own attitude and feelings—for my recovery itself. The more I accept this responsibility, the greater my freedom. I don't have to be controlled by outside forces. My perception of reality has changed and continues to change as a result of the Twelve Steps. I know that working the Steps to the best of my willingness results in a positive change for me and others. Step Twelve points out the results of working the first Eleven Steps—a continuing spiritual awakening!

54. SLIPPERY PEOPLE AND PLACES

We hear, "If you sit in the barber chair long enough, you're bound to get your hair cut," or "If you hang out with dogs, you'll get fleas."

In recovery, we stay aware and keep in contact with our Higher Power. We keep our addictions in check with our Step work. We now know the difference between what is right and wrong for us. We know we are weak and powerless over our addictions. We know it is only by the grace of our Higher Power, our meetings, our friends, that we can keep ourselves focused on recovery.

So we learn to stay away from slippery places and slippery people. We know we are always just one step away from going back out. We have learned how our wills, uncontrolled, will always look for shortcuts to happiness. When our contact with our Higher Power is weak, we begin to listen to the voices that call us back into the dark days before the Program. Our minds play tricks on us. They only let us remember the true and beautiful moments, not the dark and ugly days and nights before the Program. I've changed my playmates, playgrounds, and playthings. I will stay clear of slippery people and places.

55. EXCUSES

My recovery has helped me in many ways. Today I've been thinking about what a change I've made in my attitude around the subject of excuses. Before the Program, I used my differences as excuses. Because I wasn't good-looking enough, tall enough, rich enough, smart enough, I could get away with or not try certain things. My thinking and attitude limited my behavior and at the same time caused me to act out in negative and strange ways when I was using.

They say that the Program is "education without graduation." I've learned that escaping from reality causes more problems than trying to cooperate with life. Reality is different and difficult at times, but I now know I can't change the *facts* of life that are out of my control. I *can* change my *attitudes* toward them. It simply comes down to working on acceptance.

I've slowly been able to remove the chip on my shoulder. I work at the Program every day and remember that problems don't come my way because "life isn't fair." It's important to our recovery to remember, "We don't have attitudes; they have us." I'm learning new attitudes toward old problems, and new solutions for them, by working my Program. I am learning to live in the real world.

56. TRUE FRIENDS

One of my biggest fears coming into this Program was "what about my old friends?" The "old timers" kept telling me I'd have to give them up. I really didn't know how to make new friends, especially when I wasn't wasted. I didn't think I knew how to be a friend. It turned out that it all came pretty easily. The old friends just stopped calling. Once they knew I was in recovery, they didn't want me around. I realized then that the only thing I had in common with those people were the parties! There were one or two who did call, and I know now that those were and still are friends. They accepted me for who I am and support me one hundred percent.

I have new friends that are the same way. These are the people with whom I have shared my growth in recovery, the people I've met in treatment, meetings, conventions, and other clean and sober activities. These are friends that I can call at any hour if I need them, or they can call me. Yet we still respect each others' privacy. These are friends that don't judge me for my wrongdoings, but praise me for my accomplishments. These are friends I can trust with my feelings. They are "true friends."

57. FEAR OF THE PAST

I know I don't want to return to the way I was living eighteen months ago, before the Program. My sponsor suggests that fear of those days not be the reason I stay in recovery. Fear keeps me from being open to this new way of living. If I'm only in recovery because I'm afraid of the old way of life, I'm not paying attention to or learning about the new. It keeps me busy looking back over my shoulder to make sure the old life isn't creeping up on me. I'm stuck, not growing, and I'm blowing off opportunities I have today.

I have to want the Program out of a desire for a new life, not out of a fear of the old. Positive thinking and behavior need to be in charge if I am to make any character growth. Fear of the past encourages negative thinking right now that can harm me. Guilt and shame come from the past, just like fear. If those feelings are what drive me, I will never grow.

58. SIXTEEN AND SOBER

When I became sober at sixteen, I thought my life was over. What was I going to do with myself and all this spare time? When I was using, my biggest choices were which party to go to or how many parties I could hit in one night. Today, my choices are made differently and my time is spent in a productive way. I can honestly say that I have done more "stuff" in sobriety than I ever did when I was using, and I can even remember what I did and not have to worry about being embarrassed at school the next day.

In sobriety, my weeks are spent at meetings and doing service work. My weekends are filled with dances, ski trips, picnics, camping, and more meetings. I love every minute of it. It's hard for me to find enough time to do all the things I like to do. I can smile again without it hurting my face, I can laugh without dope, and I can cry and not feel like a wimp. I can live life without worrying about my next drink or where I was going to get my next hit. I can go to bed at night feeling good about myself and still feel good when I wake up. To me, that's **FUN**!

59. MIRACLES

It's suggested not to put yourself through any major changes in the first year of recovery. I followed that advice, but I sure had a lot of "wreckage" from my using days to deal with.

My first 90 days of sobriety were a living hell—it wasn't that much fun for me. I was looking at a minimum 90-day sentence in jail for old warrants. I was fired from my job. My girlfriend left me. I had to move back in with my parents. I owed thousands of dollars in unpaid bills, and everyone wanted their money now.

I didn't think I was ready for responsibility and reality. I thought I *liked* living life being high, drunk, and irresponsible. People started telling me I wasn't going to make it to my 90-day birthday. Being stubborn, I set out to prove them all wrong. I kept going to meetings and I didn't drink or drug in between. I kept it simple and tried not to "future trip." The one sentence I heard that helped me the most was "Don't quit five minutes before the miracle happens." That simple phrase has helped keep me in the Fellowship for two years now. Every day of my life has become a miracle.

60. SELF-ESTEEM

Self-esteem is something that everyone has. Sometimes it can be taken from you and sometimes it just takes awhile to find it. There was a time when I felt like the scum that grows around the bottom of the toilet! I had been stripped of all self-esteem and

I had no idea where to start looking for it or how. I accepted that the first thing I had to do was think clearly and the only way I could do that was to get off the booze and drugs. So I did. That made it worse! But it was a start.

All those awful things I experienced, and all those awful things I did to other people, came to the surface. Then I really felt like the "scum of the earth." I couldn't just ignore those feelings. Believe me, I tried, but they didn't go away. It's taken time, willingness, commitment, and listening to my Higher Power to learn to accept my past and forgive myself for my wrongdoings. I learned that the person who did those things wasn't me, it was my addiction taking over. Now I know that I am a caring and loving person with feelings. Slowly the pieces of self-esteem are being found and put back together. I realize it may be some time before the puzzle is finished, but for every moment I stay in recovery and continue to progress and not look for perfection, I can pat myself on the back. I **am** the most important person in my life.

61. TREATMENT WAS ONLY THE BEGINNING

One of the most important things I've found over the years is that "treatment" is such a small part of recovery. There are some people who have been through two or three treatment centers, some even more. Each time they may stay clean for awhile—maybe days, weeks, sometimes even years. It always turns out the same—relapse.

Usually it's being "set up" each day before the relapse. It starts when the meetings stop. When the "old friends" are starting to look good, and those "old places" are calling your name. It's your addiction taking over, the "devil on your shoulder" or "the monkey on your back." Either way you look at it, if you don't get it off your back, it'll get you every time. You'll be right back where you left off or worse. I've seen it happen too many times. "Stinking thinking" starts to take over. This can be easily prevented! When you think you don't need a meeting, you need to go. When other people are becoming annoying, take a look at yourself. When the "old" feelings and temptations start creeping up, remember "easy does it," and take it "one day at a time."

62. WE'RE THE FUTURE

It really bugs me when I go to a meeting and hear one of the "old timers" say those ever-so-famous words: "I've been drinking since before you were even born," or "I've spilled more drinks on my tie than you've ever drunk." Then there are the ones who feel so sorry for you, and wish there was something they could do.

Being a young person in the Program isn't easy. We have to deal with these situations. We can either let it eat at us and affect our recovery, or we can try to look to these people for guidance and learn from their knowledge and experience. We need to give the old-timers a chance to help us. Keep in mind, when you become an "old timer," how you felt when you heard those comments. After all, we are the future of our Fellowship and there will come a time when we aren't the "youngest" ones at the meeting!

63. WITHOUT RECOVERY...

Without it, I could not laugh. I only cried.
Without it, I could not trust or be trusted.
Without it, I could not love. I only hated.
Without it, I could not sleep. I only lay awake in fear
        of nightmares.

Without it, I could not smile. I only frowned.
Without it, I could not be ME.
Without it, I could not LIVE. I could only die.

64. YOUNG N.A.s

So, you are a teenager looking for recovery—
you're not alone. I got clean when I was seventeen,
almost three years ago. It seems impossible, but
believe me it's not. We can stay clean.

You may face opposition; I did. It's not as bad
as what I faced in active addiction. I am a female,
and one setback was that early on some sick fellows
tried to teach me all thirteen steps. I caught on and
chalked it up to experience. I learned who the
winners were.

Then there were the ladies. Our area didn't
have many. The not-so-healthy ones treated me like
I was a threat. No matter what I did, their attitude
wouldn't change. Funny though—ironic—those
same ladies usually didn't attend the women's group.
I was lucky. My area did have a women's group.
There I found ladies who enjoyed each other. They
became my best friends.

In the beginning I felt I had to prove I was an
addict. Nonsense. I was so sensitive. When others
said, "You were so fortunate to find the Program so

young because you didn't have to go through the hell I did," I just wanted to puke. Like my pain wasn't real? I am an addict and my pain hurt just as bad.

Then I tried service work; what a trip. Everyone thought I was a joke. I guess they believed the younger one is, the more irresponsible. It was hard changing their minds, but I did. I had to work my rear end off to prove I knew what I was doing. It worked.

One day at an Area Service Committee meeting, I confronted a man about a tradition violation. What? A youngster understanding traditions? That's right! Addicts began standing behind me, putting trust and faith in my recovery.

I think mostly so many N.A.s see us come and go so often. They might be afraid we won't make it. Honestly, a lot of teenagers don't make it. It's not just young people, it's any newcomer. Don't worry, I wasn't a newcomer forever, and every year I'm a little older. If we're done using and want recovery, "together we can."

What would the Fellowship do without us? We have an excess of energy, big ideas, wild dreams, lives to live. Our spectrums are unlimited.

One day we will be the old-timers. Just imagine the Fellowship in the year 2059. Only we can see our Platinum Anniversary. (Remember, one day at a time.)

So don't worry if you feel like I once felt. It's normal. I just didn't allow my feelings to drive me out. I appreciate the hassles I once had. It gave me a reason to try harder. If it weren't for determination and those hard times I wouldn't have my husband, my career, and hold an area chairman position.

I've made it so far!

65. EVERYDAY LIFE

Learning to accept that my recovery was only "one day at a time" was not easy. Even now, with nine months of recovery behind me, I'm still knocked out at the simple, but nonetheless extraordinary, amount of strength I achieve by keeping my life on a "one day at a time" basis.

My first attempt to join the Fellowship ended in failure because I was doing it to please my parents. So I spent another eighteen months out there on the merry-go-round of active addiction and people-pleasing and ended up in treatment. At this point, I was given the opportunity of an extensive course on the Program. That was where my recovery really started.

I had heard many times before, "take life 'one day at a time,'" but took no notice, being a stubborn, big-headed, I-know-better type. But being out of work again—through my own fault again—I was running around in circles until an older member told me, "Let go, Let God" and "one day at a time is all we have." So for a change, I really took notice and started to listen and learn what was being said at every meeting and in every conversation with members of the Fellowship. The old habits of people-pleasing, projection, and wanting everything last week had to be changed. So now I really had to start out on this path of "one day at a time." Only by constantly remembering Step Two of the Program as well, do I find for me life is really worth living again.

Although life is not always easy even now, at least I know that given these tools and listening to the advice offered, recovery from this illness with the help of my fellow members is a fact of my everyday life.

66. MY SPONSOR

When I was in the Program only a short time, it was suggested I find a sponsor, a person who had the kind of recovery I wanted. The reason for finding a sponsor was to have someone who would guide me through the 12 Steps and help me apply the tools of the Program to problems I would come across.

I finally asked a guy at my home group. I was a little hesitant because he was 40 (pretty old), and what would we have in common? But I asked him, and he agreed to be my sponsor.

I soon found out that our age difference of 18 years didn't really matter. The first time we got together, he picked me up to go have coffee. He was listening to a Def Leopard tape, which really blew me away. We talked about one of the songs on the tape, *Foolin'*. When I was using and loaded, I used to take a song and think I was singing it, that I was one of the band members, and the words were my words. That song summed up my life before recovery. "Is anybody out there? Does anybody care?" I was so full of self-pity, that was my theme song. We had a long talk about living in rock 'n roll lyrics, especially that song. So that's how my relationship with my sponsor began, and it's lasted for over two years.

I've found in recovery that there **is** "somebody out there," and I've found a sponsor and fellow members who "really care." I'm not on the pity pot any more. Sponsorship is one of the important ways of carrying the message. Sponsors share freely their experience of working the Program. They don't nag or manage our lives. At times, sponsors may appear to be very strict, but they're only trying to pass on their knowledge.

Now I'm a sponsor, and helping my sponsee also helps me. Thinking about my sponsee reminds me: I need to return his Pink Floyd tapes. Or are they my sponsor's?

67. NO LONGER AFRAID

I used to be afraid of everything and everybody: Dogs, heights, my boss, my girlfriend, the neighbors, life in general. You see, I had told myself that there are certain things I have to do and others I shouldn't even dream of doing. So all the time I was afraid I was going to do the most shameful and degrading things. I lived in constant fear, but I couldn't tell you exactly what I was afraid of. I had this general uneasiness; anxiety, I think they call it. I firmly believed that something was bound to go wrong and I would be blamed for it.

In the past, the only time this anxiety disappeared was when I got wasted. Then I became fearless. I was in charge. I became inspired. I talked. Boy, did I talk! Come tomorrow, I would be trembling and wishing I could disappear. Ashamed. Ashamed because there was no doubt in my mind that I must have done or said something awful. How can you be unafraid? Especially when **they** look at you the way they do: as though they are secretly playing back a video of all you said or did the night before!

In the first months of recovery, somebody in the Fellowship told me she wasn't afraid of anything. I believed that to be a lie. How can you be unafraid when this world is so full of **them**—yes, **them?** Those who look daggers at you. Those who give you the we-know-all-about-you look. You know, **THEM**.

This friend of mine explained to me that she can't be afraid because God is in charge of her life. Moreover, God didn't create her to torture, harass, and generally make life unpleasant for her. So why should she be unduly worried? In any case, things always happen the way they are meant to happen. In fact, accepting this basic fact is not a sign of weakness. It is actually good, practical common sense.

Since joining the Fellowship, whenever something scares or even threatens to scare me, I tell somebody immediately. This takes a lot of weight off my shoulders. I sincerely believe we were not made to carry all the problems of the world. Telling somebody helps me because I know now that there are at least four eyes that are watching this monster which is threatening to destroy me with fire and brimstone that gushes out of its gigantic nose. Actually, the monster is usually an unpaid traffic ticket or the fact that I owe two months' rent. As soon as I tell one of my friends, the problem assumes human dimensions and the monster disappears.

I'm no longer afraid of shadows. If I'm scared, I tell somebody and they explain to me that it's only a shadow. I no longer sit around and sweat blood over imaginary anxieties.

68. I AM

1. I am a unique and precious human being, always doing the best I can, always growing in wisdom and love.

2. I am in charge of my own life.

3. My first responsibility is my own growth and well-being. The better I am to me, the better I will be to others.

4. I refuse to be put down by the attitudes or opinions of others.

5. My actions may be good or bad, but that doesn't make me good or bad.

6. I make my own decisions and assume the responsibility of any mistakes. I need not feel shame about them.

7. I am not free as to the things that will happen to me, but I am 100 percent free as to the attitude I have toward these things. Whether I feel a sense of well-being or suffer depends on my attitude.

8. I do not have to prove myself to anyone. I need only express myself as honestly and effectively as I am capable.

9. I can be free of resentment.

10. My emotional well-being is dependent primarily on how much I love me.

11. I am kind and gentle toward me.

12. I live a day at a time, do first things first.

13. I am patient and serene for I have the rest of my life in which to grow.

14. Every experience I have in life, even the unpleasant ones, contributes to my learning and growth.

15. No one in the world is more important than I am.

16. My mistakes and failures do not make me a louse, a crumb, or whatever. They only prove that I am imperfect, that is, human. And there's nothing wrong with being human.

17. Once I have reconciled to God and my neighbor, I can be completely free of remorse.

69. THE YETS

The stories we hear in meetings often shock us. It seems hard to believe that some members could have harmed themselves in such ways. We hear about arrests, bankruptcies, loss of family and home, lost jobs, violence, jail, physical injury—the list goes on. Most of us said to ourselves, "I was never that bad. Maybe I don't really belong here."

Our sponsors and fellow members quickly straightened us out. We were *comparing* our histories with other members. We were told to *identify* with the stories, not compare. Some of us had been lucky that worse things hadn't happened to us while we were using. We were reminded those things hadn't happened to us "yet." If we relapsed, the "yets" were waiting.

I need to remember to identify, not compare. I don't need to relapse and go through *the Yets*.

70. TRASH

I've been thinking about a story my sponsor told me the other day. It goes like this: A man was walking down an alley, looking into trash cans and dumpsters. He glanced around each time he looked into one to see if anyone was watching, then he hastily pushed back the swinging lid and dug around in the can. He became so involved in his search that he completely disregarded any onlookers. Every few seconds he brought out an object he thought worthy of saving.

My sponsor asked me, "Are you still digging around in trash cans?" Not the trash cans along the alleys and streets, but the trash cans on different levels of life. We do find what we look for in life. The cheap, negative, and trashy things of life are always there if that's what we're looking for, but the good and the positive also exist.

The man at the trash can found what he was looking for—**trash**. I can always find it if I hunt for it. I can also find the good things in life and in people, if I choose to look for them. Recovery gives me the freedom of choice—my addiction and stinking thinking no longer make choices for me. Life is largely made up of what I seek, and whatever I look for I can usually find. This determines my choices in life.

71. RECOVERY IS NOT ...

It's not about addiction,
It's about feelings.
It's not about circumstances,
It's about acceptance.
It's not only about improvement,
It's about growth.
It's not about control,
It's about surrender.
It's not about fear,
It's about trust.
It's not about strategy,
It's about willingness.
It's not about religion,
It's about God.

It's not about rules,
It's about freedom.
It's not about judgment,
It's about love.
It's not about addiction,
It's about life.

72. EGO — GOOD VS. BAD

Ego isn't all bad. We sometimes get that impression in meetings. Ego can be a motivation to achieve, and if it is for the good of the Program as a whole, then how can it be considered a character defect?

In my case, it becomes a defect when I am right and the rest of you "out there" don't know what you are talking about. "No one understands me." That, I have come to realize, is my warning signal; my EGO has taken over. It is time for me to find a quiet place and do some soul-searching. And what I usually come up with is balance; or as the dictionary says, *"emotional equilibrium, a harmonious or satisfying arrangement."* My ego returns to normal, and you out there aren't nearly as goofy as I thought you were.

What I guess I am trying to say is: life will always be a struggle with our ego, but we can keep it manageable, if we ask ourselves the question, "Is it to make me look good, or will it benefit others more?" We are told that E.G.O. = Edging God Out.

73. WE GET WHAT WE WORK FOR

There is no magic in recovery. We get what we work for.

When I first came in, I wanted all the good things people had but I didn't want to work for them. Oh, I worked the Steps—at least the ones I thought I needed. And when it came to Steps 6 and 7, I was ready and willing to have my Higher Power remove my shortcomings—should I have any, of course. I had no idea what they were because I didn't think I needed Steps 4 and 5. But I prayed, vaguely, that should He see any shortcomings, I was ready for Him to remove them. The principle of Step 7 is humility. I had none.

As I made progress in recovery, I became aware of many character defects and of just how blind I had been to them. Mercifully, my Higher Power showed me only what I was ready to see.

I became depressed and thought I could never be forgiven for or relieved from these shortcomings. This depression, I discovered, was not humility, but another form of "playing God," believing my character defects were more powerful than my Higher Power's forgiveness.

Then, when I recognized Who had the power and who was powerless, I had to decide if I were "entirely ready" to ask Him to remove my shortcomings. After all, my character defects were what made up my personality, and I was pretty much in love with who I was. Self-will had been my HP for a lifetime. I was afraid, not knowing that something better would take the place of my character defects.

With all the honesty I was capable of at the time, I worked the Steps in order, 1 through 6, then 7, asking as humbly as I could that my Higher Power remove my shortcomings. They did not disappear. I was not struck pure.

Then I was made aware that character defects are like active addiction. I couldn't keep using and expect God to relieve my disease. Neither could I keep practicing my character defects and expect God to remove them.

I was going to have to develop a new set of habits—to work against myself—and as I practiced these new habits, the old habits/character defects would begin to die.

And so I began really living the Program, the daily striving to change, to let go and receive more. It doesn't happen overnight. It takes years of practice. I have not yet been struck pure. I am not a saint. But I claim, accept, and am grateful for spiritual progress.

74. TO MY SPONSEE

Welcome to our world. It can be filled with joy, peace, and serenity, if you let it. I'll try to help. I'm not a professional counselor or a medical consultant. I hope to be your friend. I have only my experience, strength, and hope to share. I don't have answers, but I can help you find answers. I can't keep you sober; I can only carry the message and help you find your own spirituality. I will listen and hear and learn with you. I will love you until you can love yourself—and beyond.

75. STARFISH

Early one morning I was walking down the beach as the tide was going out. I saw a man coming the other way. I noticed as he approached that he would occasionally stop, pick up a starfish stranded by the outgoing tide, look at it, then throw the starfish out into the sea.

When we met, I asked him what he was doing.

"Well, if the starfish are still on the sand when the sun comes up and hits them, they will surely die. I merely throw them back in the sea and give them a chance to live."

I responded: "But there are hundreds of miles of beach and you are just one man. Does what you are doing really matter?"

He picked up another starfish, looked at it, and threw it out into the sea. "It does to that one," he said.

I think this little story fits all of us in recovery. Aren't we all starfish on the beach? I know that I was and someone threw me back into the sea of life for one more chance. It matters to me, so now I walk the beach when the tide's going out, in search of starfish.

76. STRUGGLE KEEPS US GROWING

Sometimes we get discouraged because we seem to be constantly struggling with ourselves. We struggle "not to react" in the wrong way, against resentment or self-pity; we struggle with jealousy, with depression. Or perhaps we must struggle for a sense of acceptance and belonging, for a happier attitude, or a forgiving attitude. We wonder if we will ever be able to be what we want to be without struggling for it. And we make the mistake of supposing that the need to struggle with ourselves means that we are somehow failing, or falling short of what is required of us in spiritual growth. This is not necessarily so.

It is struggle that keeps us growing, and it is the temptation to give in to the wrong attitudes and reactions that keep us struggling, or make it necessary for us to struggle. Both temptation and struggle are part of growth and without them there could be no spiritual growth at all. The day we have no inner temptations and no struggle in ourselves to overcome them will be the day we stop growing.

77. MY GARDEN

I've been able to relate my recovery to a garden of beautiful flowers. Someone had planted the seeds, but it was up to me to surrender and begin the growing process (Step 1). In this garden, I can see the beauty of the love, compassion, caring, and sharing with others.

The sun shines down with warmth to help me and my garden grow. I see this as my Higher Power (God) and love from my fellow members and my sponsor. Then the clouds roll in—this is my pain and sorrow, and from this rain (tears) and the storms of life, my garden and I grow and flourish. After the storms pass the sun sparkles on the raindrops, and I know each time my H.P. is *always* there for me. In this I can find trust (Steps 2 and 3). My flowers cannot grow without a little fertilizer—*never* too much, because then my flowers would burn up and die. Such would be my recovery.

Then there are weeds I need to keep clearing away by doing the 4th and 5th Steps. And by doing the 10th Step daily I can try to keep the weeds of life from choking my beautiful flowers. The tools of the Program help me, for without them I would have no suggested way to keep my garden in order.

The large weeds that are stubborn and hard to get rid of I keep plugging away at "one day at a time" with Steps 6 and 7. These are my defects of character. And to make amends without becoming self-righteous. This is all part of my growing process (Steps 8 and 9). Prayer and meditation help nurture my garden every day (Step 11).

Then with time there come small seeds that are carried on the wind (voice and example) of my experience, strength, and hope of a better way of life to those who are suffering, in and out of recovery (Step 12).

Then perhaps another garden can grow and find the beauty, peace, and serenity that the Fellowship promises if I am willing to practice these principles.

But if I choose to relapse, my garden becomes as if a *nuclear bomb* had struck, barren and with no life. For then I am lost.

78. FREEDOM OF CHOICE

The door opens and you walk out into the sunshine and the light kind of blinds your eyes for a while. A lot of us are not used to having choices. We denied our problem and wanted to stay tied to the sources of our misery. As we gradually freed ourselves of compulsions, guilts, and destructive attitudes, we became aware of a new freedom we had not bargained for. We could choose. No longer were we motivated by alcohol, drugs, or the grudges and judges of the past. This was a freedom many of us were not used to, and more than once got loaded to avoid. Our disease made the decisions for us.

Today, the decisions in our lives are ours to make and we are free to make them without being pushed around by our sickness—if we choose to. The decisions in my life now are pleasant ones. There are no judges now, no irate bosses nor angry parents to dictate ultimatums. There are no creditors or police officers at my door. There is none of the old "lesser of two evils" choice-making. All the options are great. Can't lose. But frankly, I'm a little inexperienced yet at that sort of freedom. Left to my own devices, it's a proven fact I'll screw up.

I need the 11th Step just as much during the good times as I do when things are rough. There is no need to make decisions alone. There is no need to do anything alone. We learned that with Step 3. You gotta listen, and you gotta learn to be patient. Once upon a time, patience was hard for most of us, but not any more. As long as our HP is driving, I'm sure we'll get there on time. After all, our HP knows where we're going and we don't.

79. WHAT'S AGE GOT TO DO WITH IT?

In the past eight years that I've been sober, I have given a great deal of thought to having found the Program at the age of twenty-two.

I had come to a clear realization of the hope-lessness of my condition several years before, and the idea of another 20, 30, or 40 years on that path in life was unbelievably overwhelming. Seeing people around me who had reached a bitter and futile end in life and knowing that with each step I took I was heading helplessly and hopelessly to the same end, created a sense of doom that only an alcoholic or addict could understand.

But understanding I found and it came in the form of a man twice my age with many different experiences in life. The bond of identification was formed because he talked of his own sense of isolation and desperation, and it had nothing to do with what he did or how old he was. It had, however, everything to do with the disease, and I said, "That's me."

Since coming in, I have not noticed any par-ticular advantage or disadvantage with being young. I have noticed, however, that because of my age I am confronted with perhaps a different set of circum-stances than someone 20 or 30 years older. For example, because of my age (not my disease), I am confronted with questions about career, marriage, and family that an older member may have already established.

Other than circumstances such as these, I truly see no difference between myself and someone who is 16 or 60. I see more a common bond by what we are as fellow members and who we are as children of God.

80. NO GRADUATION

When I first came into these rooms, I thought I would come to learn how to stop drinking—get phone numbers of people who didn't use, so when I graduated from the "class" and went back out there, I could call someone if I wanted to drink again. I saw people in the rooms smiling and laughing and healthy-looking! I decided that these people had what I'd been praying for most of my 23 years of life.

I was disappointed about not being able to drink any more at such a young age. I wondered what I'd do at Christmas and New Year's and weddings, etc. I wondered and I listened to other recovering alcoholics—people who had lost wives/ husbands, children, businesses; people who went to prison; people who had really suffered; and I began to be grateful. I didn't have to do those things. I didn't have to go through that. I knew that I had better pay attention to these people and what they were saying to me. I learned that alcoholism is a progressive disease, so those things could happen to me if I continued to drink.

I began to see the gift that my Higher Power was giving me—my 12 Step Program, the people, the honesty and love, and the true friendships that are made. I was overwhelmed by it all and I decided that this would become a way of life for me. Thank God, we don't have to graduate here. I'm lucky that I'm young and was able to see what alcohol was doing to me. I'm very grateful to be a member of Alcoholics Anonymous at my age.

81. NO LONGER LIVE IN FEAR

I started drinking and using when I was ten years old. By the time I was sixteen, I was in situations a sixteen-year-old shouldn't have been in—juvenile halls, court-ordered psychiatry, stealing to support my "habits," fights. When I was eighteen, I lived in a car. Twenty years old, I woke up Christmas day in a straitjacket, not knowing how I got there. Blackout, as usual. My eyes showed no life. I had knots in my stomach all the time and I was scared. All the while, I wasn't growing emotionally or spiritually.

I've been in the Program three years now, and I look and feel younger than I did when I was using. I work the same Twelve Steps as anybody else in the Program and my life has changed. The knots in my stomach have untied. I get scared at times but I no longer live in fear. I have a God of my understanding who shows me the way out, without taking anything. Recovery has given me a way of life that works.

I am young and growing in the Fellowship.

82. SOMETHING IN COMMON

Down the street there is a party going on. Everyone is celebrating the end of summer and the beginning of school. I can hear kids yelling and laughing as they stumble down the street toward their dorms or frat houses. Last fall, that would have been me . . . laughing and stumbling. Mostly stumbling. Trying to make it home to bed so I knew where I was when I attempted to get up to make it to classes. It seems ironic now that we prepared to start school, the place where we use our brains, by numbing them with alcohol.

Drinking in college is a very acceptable way to meet people and be "a part of" the school's social life—for some. It no longer is for me because I am an alcoholic. I haven't been drinking for as long as most of my fellow members, but we have something in common that goes beyond age: pain and the desire to end it.

Before college, in high school and even junior high for that matter, I never used drugs and alcohol like other people. They played with them; I *needed* them. To feel comfortable, to make friends, to feel important, I felt that I needed to be loaded. Now I feel all those things in recovery. I knew I could easily spend another ten or twenty years deciding when I would stop drinking and using—but I don't have to. I don't want to.

Since I've been in the Fellowship, I've met people even younger than myself who have had lower bottoms. I take them and their sobriety as seriously as anyone else's, perhaps more so, because I know what it is like to walk into a meeting and be the youngest person there. The biggest surprise was to realize that being young really doesn't matter, because everyone in these rooms has something in common in spite of age—the pain and the desire to make it end.

83. WHAT CHARACTER DEFECTS?

I went to a meeting the other night and the topic was (ugh!) Character Defects and what to do about them. Boy, could I feel the heat rising. When I first came to the Program I didn't think there was anything wrong with me except the fact that I got wasted and I usually got into trouble as a result of it. Did they clear that up for me in a hurry! My life was a mess. I couldn't do much of anything right and I sure didn't like myself. I had to admit that I had a drinking problem. Gone was some of the false pride. I had to ask for help to stay sober. Gone was some of the inflated ego. I had to get honest with myself. Gone was some of the dishonesty. This is great. It really works. I can go to a meeting and some of my Character Defects just get better. They don't go away completely but if I keep coming back everyone promises that things will get better.

Funny thing happened a couple of days later. I went to a meeting and the topic was on character building and assets. That was a switch. They wanted to know what I was doing right and what I liked about myself. Nobody ever cared about that before the Program. The best part was that I started caring about myself and I could really see things about myself that were good. Isn't it amazing what the Program can do for a person that doesn't have a lot of hope left when they first walk through the doors? They make them feel worthwhile and they make them believe that they are worth saving. I don't know about you, but I am going to keep coming back. There are a lot of nice people in the meetings that keep asking us to. Nobody ever did that before.

84. HOW TO QUIT PLAYING GOD

1. Offer no advice unless it's asked for.
2. Listen to other people's dreams and help them in the way they wish to be helped.
3. Encourage them to find their own strength.
4. Reserve judgment at all times.
5. Admit that you don't know all the answers.
6. Build confidence in the other person until their judgment becomes clear.
7. Dwell on the right instead of the wrong.
8. Have faith in the wisdom of the Program.
9. Look for the good in each person. Respect it.
10. Never discount the other person's good intentions.

85. **FEAR OF CHANGE**

As alcoholics and addicts, we all have that fear of change. But we all must change, because it is a part of our recovery program. If we don't change, we're going to relapse or be miserable in the Program. We're only one drink, toke, hit, away from being back out there.

The fear of admitting that we are powerless, the fear of sharing our feelings with others in the Program—to let them know who we are—are big fears for us. The fear of acceptance is another big one. We can change all this with the help of the Program—the Twelve Steps, our sponsors, and our fellow members.

When we change, we're not losing anything, we're gaining a lot. The Program has a lot to offer.

There are different types and ways we need or can change—like the places we once went to. Or the people we used to get loaded with, who were our so-called friends; and we even change the activities we used to participate in. But most of all, we have to change ourselves: not so much on the outside, but it's what's on the inside that counts—that which we all lost during our active addiction. We're talking about what's in our hearts—gut level change.

We can even ask our Higher Power for the courage to help us with these changes. That's a change in itself: having and believing in a Higher Power, a Power greater than ourselves. And we no longer believe in our drug of choice that started out being our "friend." We no longer have to face reality or change all by ourselves; we have help now.

Accept the changes and accept yourself. You'll find you're a better person and like yourself more. And others will too!

86. AM I BEING HONEST?

We've heard around the tables that this is an honest Program. And it is! Before coming into the Program we were liars, cheaters, and generally all-around dishonest. Then we began recovery, found out that it is an honest Program, found out that it was time to start getting honest, and started to grow when we got honest with ourselves, our Higher Power, and other people.

It's been said that in order to get honest with others, we must get honest with ourselves first. How are we going to be honest with others or with ourselves? Tough question, isn't it? We learn it one day at a time—just like everything else. If we want this Program to work for us, honesty plays a big part in our recovery and we cannot "skip over it."

A big part of honesty is being honest about the Program, knowing that we can't work it on our own because our way didn't work. We need the help of sponsors and the Twelve Steps, and most of all we need our Higher Power. All we have to do is reach out and ask, and that unconditional love the Fellowship has will be there for us. But nobody can reach out for us; we have to do it ourselves!

Steps Four and Five help us get a lot of honesty. That's when we get rid of all the garbage (if we're honest) and clean house, so to speak. There's no such thing as "perfect honesty." The best we can do is to work and strive for a better way or quality of honesty. Honesty with ourselves and others will help us stay and grow. So let's stop and ask ourselves, "Am I being honest with myself and others?"

87. FOR TODAY ONLY

There are two days in every week about which we should not worry, two days which should be kept from fear and apprehension.

One of these days is **Yesterday**, with its mistakes and cares, its faults and blunders, its aches and pains. Yesterday has passed forever beyond our control.

All the money in the world cannot bring back yesterday. We cannot undo a single act we performed; we cannot erase a single word we said. Yesterday is gone.

The other day we should not worry about is **Tomorrow**, with its possible adversaries, its burdens, its large promise and poor performance. Tomorrow is beyond our immediate control. Tomorrow's sun will rise. Until it does, we have no stake in tomorrow, for it is yet unborn.

This leaves only one day: **Today**. Anyone can fight the battles of just one day. It is only when you and I add the burdens of those two awful eternities—yesterday and tomorrow—that we break down.

It is not the experience of today that drives people crazy. It is resentment or bitterness for something which happened yesterday, and the fear of what tomorrow may bring. Let us, therefore, live but *one day at a time*.

88. PLEASE LISTEN TO WHAT I'M NOT SAYING

Don't be fooled by me. Don't be fooled by the face I wear. For I wear a mask; I wear a thousand masks I am afraid to take off, and none of them are me.

I give you the impression that I'm secure, that confidence is my name and coolness my game, that the water's calm and I'm in command, and that I need no one. But don't believe me. Please.

My surface may seem smooth—underneath I dwell in confusion, in fear, in aloneness. But I hide this. I panic at the thought of my weakness and fear being found out. That's why I frantically create a mood to hide behind, a calm, sophisticated front to shield me from the glance that knows. But such a glance is my salvation and I know it. It's the only thing that can assure me of acceptance and love. I'm afraid you'll think less of me, that you'll laugh. Laughter would kill me.

So I play my game, my desperate pretending game, with a front of "having it together," and a trembling child within. And so my life becomes a front. I chatter to you in a cool tone; I tell you everything that's nothing and nothing of what's everything, of what's crying within me. So when I go into my routine do not be fooled by what I am saying. Please listen to what I'm not saying.

I dislike the phony game I'm playing. I'd like to be real and spontaneous, and me. You've got to hold out your hand even when it may seem to be the last thing I want, or need. Only you can call me into aliveness. Each time you're kind and gentle, and encouraging, each time you try to understand because you really care, my heart begins to grow wings—small wings, very feeble wings.

I want you to know how important you are to me, how you can be a creator of the person that is me if you choose to. But it will not be easy for you. A long time of feeling inferior builds strong walls.

The nearer you approach me, the harder I may strike back. It is irrational, but I **am** irrational. I fight against the very things I cry out for. But I am told that love is stronger than walls, and therein lies my hope. Please try to beat down those walls with firm hands, but with gentle hands—for a child is very sensitive.

Who am I, you may wonder? I am someone you know very well. I am every newcomer you meet.

89. WISHES FOR THE NEWCOMER

May you find serenity and peace in a world you may not always understand. May the pain you have known and the conflict you have experienced give you the strength and courage to stay in recovery, facing each new situation with courage and hope. Always know that there are those whose love and understanding will always be there, even when you feel most alone. May you discover enough goodness in others to believe in the goodness in you. May a kind word, a reassuring touch, and a warm smile be yours every day, and may you give these gifts as well as receive them. Remember the sunshine when the storm seems unending. Teach love to those who know hate, and let that love help you make spiritual progress.

May the teachings of your sponsor become part of you, so that you may call upon them and pass them on. Remember, those whose lives you have touched and who have touched yours are always a part of you, even if the encounters were less than you would have wished. May you not become too worried with material things, but instead place value on the goodness in your heart. Find time in each day to see beauty and love in the world around you. Realize that each person has abilities, but each of us is different in our own way.

What you may feel you lack in one area may be more than compensated for in another. What you feel you lack in the present may become one of your strengths in the future. May you see your future as one filled with promise and possibility. Learn to view everything as a worthwhile experience. May you find enough inner strength to determine your own worth by yourself, and not be dependent on another's judgment of your accomplishments. May you always feel welcome and loved.

90. HOW WILLING AM I?

I have "become willing" so many times in my recovery, I couldn't possibly count them all. Every time that I do, the end result is that I grow and I get better. By becoming willing I mean I become willing to do the things that are necessary for me to stay clean, be happy, and be useful to others.

The most frequent way that I use to become willing to work the Steps, to study the literature, to do an institution meeting, or whatever, is that I put myself in the position to experience an uncomfortable pain. I decided to try the Program again after going out and ending up trying to commit suicide because I had no other option to make the pain stop. Since that time I have thought suicidal thoughts in recovery only from time to time. This is due to my warped sense of thinking.

I have tried suicide only once in recovery. It was due to a lot of pain and things weren't going my way. However, it was mostly due to the fact that I was sitting on my progress. I was not doing those things that I needed to do to stay happy and useful. At that time I kicked God out of my life and took things into my own hands and retired from the Program. Then God sent me someone to help, even though I had just cussed him out. I hated this person but still he saved my life that day by taking me to a meeting I had no intention of going to. From that point on I have never been choosey on where help comes from.

I once again "became willing" to get into the Program and work the Steps. The one thing I remember every day is how bad I hurt that day. I never want the pain to become that great again, so it takes less and less to make me "become willing" today.

91. WHAT I'VE LEARNED

I've learned how to channel anger in the right direction and not take it out on myself or on others. There is no way that I can justify it enough to pick up. When I get on my little "Pity Pot" I have to stop and think is this worth relapsing over? No! Be thankful for what my Higher Power has given me.

I no longer need to lie and put on any phony fronts. People now accept me for what I am but, most important, I accept myself.

Everything does not have to go my way or be what I want it to be. My way wasn't too hot to begin with. This way of life is much better.

I have many more choices now when I am troubled. There are meetings, my sponsor, fellow members, and most of all my Higher Power. I don't have to suffer the mental pain alone. When I share it with someone else, the burden is lightened. Keeping busy has given me a good many days in recovery. Early on in the Program I was told to get involved. Well, I did as I was told and I cannot really tell you all the many benefits that I have been given. My time spent in service has helped me so much.

I can't get wasted if I don't pick up. By not getting wasted I will not regain all the misery and guilty feelings I had for many years.

Recovery has given me what nothing else has been able to: the will to go on with life, the tools which are the 12 Steps to deal with life on a daily basis.

The Program has saved my life. On many days before, I did not think it was worth saving. Recovery comes first because without it, I have nothing.

92. THINGS DON'T GET BETTER; WE GET BETTER

How often have I heard at meetings that if I stick with the Program "things will get better." At a recent anniversary celebration, a speaker, recounting the difficulties he had experienced during the first months of his recovery and how, since then, his circumstances had constantly improved, said, "and it keeps getting better."

Yet how many times have I heard it said that "things don't get better; **we** get better"?

Where is the tie-in between these two different ideas?

For me it is expressed in the Serenity Prayer, asking God to grant me serenity to accept the things I cannot change, the courage to change the things I can, and having (or relying on friends in the Program to provide) the wisdom to know the difference between the two.

In my life "things" have not really changed much. All the potential hassles at work, at home, with authority figures, or on the freeway, are all still there. I'm fairly confident that if I changed jobs, or cities, or schools, they would not disappear. They seem to be facts of life; that is, things I cannot change.

Nevertheless, in recovery, I am able, with God's grace, to handle most of these "things." They **seem** better because I don't turn a moment of anger into a no-win battle with authority; an argument with my parents isn't likely to get me thrown out of their house; nor does a mistake (my own or another's) turn into an "I'm right, you're wrong" competition.

I can see this in other ways, too. For example, my home life seems better because I no longer blame my parents for my misery. I'm more comfortable in school since I realized that "they" (the system, the bureaucracy, the teachers) were not out to get me. In neither case have "things" changed, but my attitudes, outlooks, and my expectations have.

93. ATTITUDE

Right at the beginning of Chapter 6, in the Big Book, it states we have been trying to get a new attitude, a new relationship with our Creator. The dictionary defines attitude as *"habitual mental reaction, or point of view."*

Take whichever definition you wish, but I know that for a long period of time while I was using, I did not have a good attitude toward life, school, my family, anyone, or anything. We really make life very difficult for ourselves, our family, or for anyone with whom we come in contact.

Somehow we seemed to get accustomed to looking at life through our disease. It certainly warped our point of view. We got a very warped point of view and this was reflected in our judgment. Clear-headed thinking was something we didn't have.

As long as we continue to have a bad attitude in recovery, we are not going to make or keep friends. We, for the most part, will continue to be selfish people trying to grasp happiness for ourselves and not worrying too much about others, little realizing that we are not going about gaining happiness the right way.

We have to realize, sooner or later, that we will never attain happiness until we get a new attitude, one that is not run by selfish standards, but one that considers other people and their needs and desires.

Most people really want to be happy, but they go about things the wrong way, not realizing that the way to find happiness is to stop thinking so much of themselves and to put others and their needs first.

When you see a fellow member with a good attitude, it does not necessarily mean that they have always had it. Possibly they saw where they were wrong long ago, and started working at it, one day at a time, with help from their Higher Power.

It is not easy to develop a new attitude, not thinking always of ourselves, but considering and thinking first of others and how we may be of help. It cannot be done overnight, but it is possible, if we stick to it and if we ask our Higher Power to help us.

It is the way to true happiness.

94. THE YOUNG MAN ALONE

The young man is alone. He may be riding with someone, he may be using the transits, someone may be with him, but he is alone. His whole life is only about getting and using drugs. Though he may hurt his friends, family, and loved ones, most of all he hurts himself. He lives to use; he uses to live. He lives his life, an unmanageable life, on his own terms.

He thinks he has all the power, and minute by minute he does his own will. His disease is like that of every suffering addict, but in his disease he thinks he is the only one.

A Power greater than himself got this young man to a program of recovery. Its name is Narcotics Anonymous. He had to keep coming back until he wanted it. He had to get honest with himself, be open-minded, and become willing to try. He simply kept coming back, "just for today," until the miracle happened and he stayed.

He has been clean all day today. He worked the Twelve Steps, and practiced these principles in all his affairs.

He is learning to live life on life's terms, working the Steps to the best of his ability. Now, he's a recovering addict. He doesn't want more drugs more often, he wants more recovery.

He needs only the Fellowship to recover from this disease. He's never alone, and he never has to use again. This Power greater than himself that got him to this Program is always here for him. As long as he follows this way of life, he has nothing to fear.

The young man alone now has friends. He is grateful for his faith in God and in himself. The young man alone now has real friends, and a real friend in himself.

95. WHERE I CAME FROM

I was seventeen years old. Already I had been on the streets for six years. I had become the very thing in life that I hated the most, an alcoholic. Like mother, like daughter? I was terrified because I didn't understand how or even why it happened. I was too young!

When I attended my first meeting, I already knew a lot of you. After meetings you came into the coffee shop where I worked each night. You smiled, you laughed, you glowed. I resented you and feared you. You held happiness in your hearts and I held emptiness. And you were all so much older than I, so what could we possibly offer each other? How would you ever be able to understand me?

But a tragedy brought desperation on and at the suggestion of one of you who knew me quite well, I went to a meeting. I was terrified of people in general and didn't know how I'd ever survive in a room full of strangers for an hour.

I walked in and was stunned! You welcomed me with warmth and love. I was handed a cup of coffee and shown a seat. You dedicated that first meeting to me! You shared with me your experience, strength, and hope. You shared your real feelings with me that night. I found I could understand you and you understood me as no one ever had before.

After the meeting, there were heart-felt hugs and handshakes. You even asked me to "please come back." I felt like I had finally found a place to belong to, a home. I had finally found hope for myself in you.

My sobriety back then was a real struggle. I fought myself a lot, only to lose. I never could manage to stay sober and clean for more than nine months at a time. But I kept attending meetings (even while abusing) and you were always patient with me and understanding. You always had time for me.

I noticed, too, that it wasn't just me you treated this way. It was any newcomer or old-timer who walked through your doors. I wasn't jealous, for I saw that there was enough of what you gave to encompass the universe. Seeing you made me want to give of myself.

You were literally a dream come true for me. You didn't care what kind of clothes I wore. It didn't matter that I smoked and swore diligently. Sometimes I was the class clown in meetings. You were always patient; you accepted me as I was on any given day. My questions were never termed as "stupid" and you always tried to answer as best you could. My tendency to be the "prodigal child," which you so fondly called me, never once brought about a single "I told you so" from anyone. You never condemned me; you only embraced me in the spirit of the Fellowship and said, "Let's try again."

I hated authority figures and rules. You only made suggestions and shared yourselves with me. You never once stood in judgment of me or my actions.

There was no sense of God in my life. We had abandoned each other at the age of twelve. But I learned from you that it was I who had moved and you showed me how to find Him again—a God of my very own understanding with Whom I could have a working relationship.

Your ways amazed me! I had no idea of what made you work, or who you were. So I began a desperate search for the answer not only to you, but to myself. I needed to know why I was an alcoholic and what that meant.   And then one night my sponsor handed me a small white wallet-sized pamphlet and said, "Read." Well, I did, and the light bulb went on over my head and I found answers, and a part of me found peace that night.

That was ten years ago. Things sure aren't what they used to be! I'm different today. I finally got tired of bouncing on my head and through your doors after six and a half years. Well, some are sicker than others! And each day I thank my God for the sobriety I now tenderly hold, and pray that I will continue to grow, one day at a time.

96. PUTTING MYSELF FIRST

About fourteen months ago, I got out of my seven-week treatment center. I thought life was great. I was sober and my mother and I actually got along for the first time. I thought my life was going to go the way I wanted it to. I was in a relationship with someone who was using, and I got out of that as was suggested. I then got into a sober relationship because I thought that was okay. He had one and half years of sobriety, and was such a powerful example to me. He told me how to do things, and I did them because I thought that was right. And this is how it went for six months.

I never knew other people besides his friends. We were always together. I went to his meetings. I never joined a group or got active. I did not go to any discussion or Step meetings. He told me to get a sponsor and I did. I never used her. I used him as a sponsor. I thought my sobriety was great. But my home life was not healthy. My mom and I fought all the time. She kicked me out of the house several times. At this time, my mom was eleven months into the Program. Things got worse. I never talked about how I was feeling. I was hurting real bad, and I didn't even know it. He and I were both very possessive. Things between us started falling apart.

He finally broke up with me and I was hurting real bad. I felt I had no one. I had given up all my old friends and I had never met any people on my own. I had a choice: go back out or start to help myself. I decided to help myself. With the few people I did meet on my own, I started to open up. I joined a group and got active. I went on service commitments, spoke for the first time, and went to discussion and Step meetings. I got a sponsor. My mom and I were getting along good. I felt so strong. But in a way, I was not healthy. I had an obsession with my ex-boyfriend. I called his house just to hear his voice. I followed him and did really sick things. Things turned around and got better for me. My sponsor helped me through a lot of pain. I started to let go for the first time. Just when I thought the pain was getting easier to deal with, he came back into my life. We started talking and then started going out. I was nine months sober and thought I could handle it. In one week I saw my obsessiveness kick in. He had changed a lot in four months, I thought. I wanted what we used to have. All I wanted to do was to be with him. One week later, he broke up with me again. I hurt more now than ever. I felt I was back where we had started, but the one thing I did have was the knowledge of how to really let go.

I'm seventeen years old and sixteen months sober. I got active in my group and went to a lot of meetings. I spoke and shared my feelings and the pain. These are the things I need to do to stay healthy and, most important, sober.

I still miss my boyfriend very much, but I must put myself first. I cannot put anyone in front of me or I will be a very sick person. I still think about him and what it would be like if we got back together again. But for today, we are not together and that is okay. Even if we never get back together, I can accept that. I have myself and my sobriety. My Higher Power was with me through all this pain, even at times when I doubted His will for me. I am grateful for Him, my sponsor, and the friends I made through this Program.

97.   LIVING THE N.A. PROGRAM

Just for today my thoughts will be on my recovery, living and enjoying life without the use of drugs.

Just for today I will have faith in someone in N.A. who believes in me and wants to help me in my recovery.

Just for today I will have a Program. I will try to follow it to the best of my ability.

Just for today through N.A. I will try to get a better perspective on my life.

Just for today I will be unafraid, my thoughts will be on my new associations, people who are not using and who have found a new way of life. So long as I follow that way, I have nothing to fear.

98. HOW TO EAT ELEPHANTS!

Putting things off is a hard habit to break. It's easy to ignore small problems, routine responsibilities, and everyday challenges. The trouble is, the longer you ignore them (procrastinate), the bigger they get, and pretty soon they're elephants!

Taking care of elephants is expensive—it takes a lot of time and effort. Elephants aren't house pets—they make a real mess in your "living" room. And once you let them in the house, there's no elbowroom for anything else.

In the old days before recovery, we got used to living with elephants. We didn't feel comfortable without two or three of them crowding us. We even used them to hide behind—telling ourselves our problems (elephants) were too big for us to even begin to deal with, so we just got loaded and forgot about them. We procrastinated and let them grow.

The only way to get those elephants out of our space is to nibble them down to size. We have to take "one bite at a time"—and then another, and another, until they're small enough to shove out the back door!

99. S.O.B.E.R.

I learned early in recovery that I not only had a drug and drinking problem, I also had a *thinking* problem. When I was using, I was living as two people, in two different realities. One reality was caused by my active addiction—the mood-changing chemicals I was putting into my body. The longer I used, the more my thinking turned to far-out fantasy. It was impulsive crazy, which led to compulsive acting out.

I see things clearer now, three years into recovery. Before, my Serenity Prayer went like this: "God grant me the total power to control, manipulate, and change the people, places, and things that don't agree with me and my way of thinking, and if you don't like it, screw you." My reality and behavior were controlled by drugs. I was a selfish, self-centered addict, thinking only of myself and where I could get my next high.

Recovery has helped my confused thinking. I've slowly been able to accept reality. Early on in the Program, I heard that S.O.B.E.R. meant "Son Of a Bitch, Everything's Real."

I didn't really need to understand how the Program would help me live in reality; all I had to do was follow directions. We hear around these rooms that our Fellowship doesn't teach us how to handle our using. It teaches us how to handle our recovery (reality), which is what none of us could handle in the first place, and was one of the reasons we used.

These last three years of clean time I haven't used, I've taken inventories, I've made amends, and I've prayed. I'm learning and growing up (ugh!), and now know as a fact that the more I surrender to the realities of living, the more serenity (peace of mind) I have.

100. HEADBANGER

I bounced around between recovery and using for awhile before I woke up and asked myself, "How bad does it have to get before I want to get better?" I've come from darkness into light, from believing in the devil to believing in God. I still like loud music, and I still think of myself as a "head-banger," but the lyrics are just words now, not the way I live my life. I don't let myself be controlled by negative, destructive thoughts.

One of the most important things I've learned in my two years of recovery is how to deal with anger. I think the reason I relapsed so much was because I didn't know how to deal with it before. When I got angry, there was no middle ground—I just wanted to fight. Resentments were the fuel that drove my life.

I still get angry, but the Steps have given me a way of working through it. I've learned that what fuels most of my anger is fear. When I deal with my fear, it dissolves anger. My sponsor tells me the remedy for fear is faith. When I replace anger with faith and take my inventory, my anger is reduced.

101. READY FOR A RELATIONSHIP?

The common advice given to newcomers is to wait a year before getting involved in a relationship or making any major decision. This advice is based on years of experience fellow members have had in recovery.

While this is usually a very good guideline, it's also true that the quality of our recovery can't be measured by the number of days in the Program. Most of us learn to follow advice and direction, and to work the suggestions given—except those we don't like! Then we learn the hard way.

Relationships are a very serious matter. Sexual obsessing and frustrations lead a lot of people away from the Program and back out the door, or cause them to get stuck so they don't make any progress in recovery. We hear and read a lot about love, sex, unhealthy dependency, and self-seeking. They should not be ignored.

My sponsor gave me the following list of suggestions to go over, to help me decide if I were ready for an honest relationship:

1. Do you respect yourself enough to respect another person?

2. Are your ideas about relationships and being happy in a relationship based on fantasy ideas that you have seen in movies and on television?

3. Do you pray every day?

4. Have you done a Fourth Step inventory?

5. Have you completed Step Five?

6. Do you have a sponsor you can talk to openly and honestly about everything?

7. What does your sponsor think about this?

8. Do you take regular Tenth Step inventories to see if your ideas about sex and relationships are realistic?

9. Have you been overly selfish and manipulative in past involvements? Have you changed these behaviors?

10. Do you enter relationships with high expectations?

11. Do you just want to be in a relationship so you look more "together," or are you willing to work hard at a relationship?

12. Do you want to be in a relationship with someone who may not be the type of person that's good for you, just to be rebellious again?

13. Do you depend on others for all your happiness?

14. Have you learned how to be alone with yourself without feeling lonely?

15. Do you have a better understanding of the differences between lust, love, and wishful thinking?

16. If a relationship suddenly falls apart, can you stay in recovery and not use it as an excuse for a relapse?

102. DON'T GIVE UP

If there's one thing I want to pass on to those who are struggling in recovery, it's "don't give up." Like me, a lot of people come into the Program after spending most of their lives "giving up," running away from situations that were too painful or required too much effort. It was easier to quit and find fault with things we didn't like.

It's easy to give up on a problem too quickly. A long effort at finding a solution is sometimes painful and irritating. But we learn by working the 12 Steps that the answers do come if we continue to do the research—through study and prayer, one day at a time.

Courage is what makes us do the right thing even when we want to give up. We can find happiness while surrounded by darkness; we can be kind in the middle of hate and jealousy; we can have peace of mind when we're surrounded by confusion, fear, and anger. What has helped me is knowing and remembering that there isn't much I can't handle today that my Higher Power, fellow members, and myself can't handle together.

I'm not a quitter or a loser any more.

103. REAL WORLD, REAL PAIN, REAL RECOVERY

I know that I never again (and especially today) have to handle any problem, hassle, fear, or joy alone. Learning to share the unmanageable thoughts in my head, however stupid they seem, stops them from getting any larger. Sharing the crazy and stupid with someone else gives me the ability to laugh at myself. By sharing these thoughts and hearing other people's feedback, I am not alone any more.

During recovery, I have at times held onto thoughts and let my stinking thinking control me. The thoughts become fantasies and I then find myself disappointed with my life. Today, I want to live in the real world. I don't want to wear a mask and say "I'm fine" when I'm not. It's not always easy to put my feelings into words, but today I am willing to try, however mixed up the words sound. I'm letting people in to see the real me—and I'm getting to know myself, too. I have enough faith in the Fellowship, and a little more in myself each day, to know that whatever I share won't freak people out or make them reject me. This is friendship and understanding. This Fellowship accepts people as they are, defects and all.

There's still some fear of rejection and of people thinking I'm a little weird, but as my self-esteem improves, I don't mind quite so much what others think of me. It's what I feel and think about myself that counts.

I'm on the recovery road. There's acceptance to come and still lots of change and pain. I've made it 19 months on the journey so far, but I've never had to do it alone. The more I let people into my recovery, the more I'm able to recover. It's me that has to put the work into it, but all of you make it possible.

I couldn't and can't recover alone. Thank you all for being there.

104. LIVING MY AMENDS

I had felt so guilty for so long that I really wanted to start making amends. I threw myself into some amends before I even really knew what Step Nine was all about.

The people I had hurt the most, and over the longest time, were my parents. I felt very bad about my performance as a son, but like a lot of us, I wanted immediate forgiveness, in full, the instant the first words of apology were out of my mouth. I soon had my first lesson in this being an ongoing process. While everyone was delighted that I *seemed* to be doing something about my addiction, there had been many other promises, "I'm sorries," and attempts which had been blown off. I quickly understood that staying in recovery itself was the most important thing with which I could repay these people whom I had hurt and disappointed for many years. For my parents, that was all they wanted. It would take a while to rebuild trust between us.

I've learned I have to show by *actions* as well as *words* that I honestly want to make amends where possible. As long as I stay and work my Program one day at a time, I will have time enough to show by my actions that I am sorry for the pain I caused.

105. GRATITUDE TAKES PRACTICE

Gratitude is not an emotion I've been able to feel at every moment throughout recovery. I think that gratitude is a feeling which has grown within me through my efforts in working the Program to the best of my ability. That ability has improved with practice. My sponsor told me to begin my "attitude of gratitude" by slowly counting my blessings. I was in the Program for two years before I could be grateful that I was clean and sober.

When I first came in I was glad there were people who understood the way I felt, but once I stopped using and was left with the confusion, fears, and problems, I was anything but grateful.

Today I can look back and feel grateful to the Program and fellow members for showing me the way to look within myself, sort out my character defects, and change my attitudes. By doing this I've been able to feel a new freedom come into my life.

I can feel grateful right this minute for the screwed-up life I had before coming in. Because I experienced active addiction and all the negative emotions that go with it, I have something to compare with the life I have today. I don't feel sorry for myself or like a victim any more. Today I feel freed from most of the fears I had. Loneliness has been replaced by friendships. Anxieties and conflicts have been replaced by long periods of peace of mind.

My gratitude extends to all the members who got me involved in service, as this has helped me feel part of the Fellowship. Members who had been around awhile showed me how their involvement helped them, and made me understand that if I wanted what they had, I'd better try to follow their example.

During my first months in recovery, I didn't believe it when members said they were grateful. But I can now say I love the way my life is today.

There's a lot of work to do, but if I keep trying, I know it can only get better.

106. STUPID, BORING, AND SAD

In my early days in the Program, when the fog was clearing from my brain, one of my biggest worries was that without my drugs I'd turn into a person who was stupid, boring, and sad.

More than a year later, I can now see that it was when I was *using* that I was stupid, boring, and sad. When I think about my first year of using, in my early teens, I remember loud laughter, loss of inhibitions, putting up with creepy guys, playing music at a deafening volume, joining in on practical jokes, and giving my opinions on world problems I knew nothing about.

As the disease progressed and took hold, I remember "chasing the good times," trying so hard to figure out the perfect combination of drugs to make me feel "just right." I remember trying desperately to control the high that would show everybody how together and smart I was, or ending up sitting quietly, afraid to join in the discussion in case I said something stupid—or worse, couldn't talk at all.

When my disease really established itself, I really became stupid, boring, and sad. Stupid and boring when I went on and on about how depressed I was and how life wasn't fair, sad when I looked at the regrets and the guilt I felt about my crazy behavior.

So is being in recovery stupid, boring, or sad as I feared? You know the answer just like I do. The answer is no. Recovery has given me a brain that works, plenty to do, and a happiness I never had before.

107. PLANNING OR FUTURE TRIPPING

From trying not to think about getting loaded one minute at a time, I progressed to the point of surviving twenty-four hours at a time without the constant effort of keeping those thoughts out of my mind. I started to get it through my thick head that there's a lot more to the Program than just not using.

Up until then, I hadn't really understood that living without the drugs (and in my case, alcohol too) was also about beginning to change my attitudes.

I wanted to get well instantly. I tended to be resentful if, on some days, my progress in recovery was standing still and even sliding backwards. Keeping my thoughts away from the past and the future during a given day helped to improve on this situation, and breaking the day down into smaller pieces helped even more. I can't hope ever to completely rid myself of thinking about the past or future, but these days, I feel I have them within manageable limits.

It took awhile to understand the difference between planning and future tripping. Today I spend far less time fantasizing about a great future, and I stop my thinking before I get too far off track. When I have those future thoughts going around and around in my head, I take a break for a few minutes and list my day's objectives in order of priority. I'm better off planning for the future by doing the work each day. I remember to get to a meeting when I'm future tripping.

A day is rarely all bad or all wonderful, but if I can learn to enjoy the reality of each minute as it comes along, I think perhaps I may be getting past another hurdle in my recovery.

108. FULL-TIME MEMBER

I have been in and out of the Program over the last three years. My longest time in was eight months, only to go out and do it my way and end up in trouble again.

Was half a can of beer ever enough? Or half a joint, or half a line of coke? I always needed the whole thing and more. So why has it taken me so long to understand that just a little bit of the Program now and then would be no use to me?

Why? Because I went to meetings and listened without hearing. I picked meetings that fit around what I wanted to see on T.V. I just gave the Program lip service. I had never given it my whole self.

It's a few months since my last relapse, and I have been to as many meetings as I could. For once, I'm taking the Program home with me, and there's a big difference. I've been a full-time member, in and out of the meetings, doing what is suggested to get better. I keep asking myself two questions: If I really believe I am powerless and a Higher Power and the Program can help me, why not accept it? Why not give it a chance where I had failed? Because all I have to lose by working the Program full-time is the pain and misery of a part-time member.

109. RECOVERY BEHIND BARS

I am very new to A.A. and a young alcoholic—twenty years old. I am just about to be let out of jail.

My drinking life was about the same as most of you, but in my first attempt at recovery I had my problems. I went to my first meeting a few years ago, when I came back home after a four-week bender and felt like death warmed over. I came to A.A., got a sponsor, and tried, but my heart wasn't in it. I still felt that I could drink. After about seven weeks of going to meetings, I tried to take my life. Then I went through Christmas dry. I wasn't sober, just dry, and I hated it—a week after Christmas I went on a binge and ended up getting arrested. I was then let out on bail and had to go to court about a month later. It took six months for me to finally get sentenced. Those six months were hell. It was relapse after relapse and back to the Program full of guilt. I knew that I needed help but could not seem to stop.

I blamed family, police, courts, friends, relatives, and nearly everything but myself, and that was the problem; I hadn't accepted that I was powerless over alcohol. I thought that the reason I drank was because my life was a mess. I know now that it was the other way around.

I got sentenced to eighteen months. I remember sitting in the cell crying my eyes out and wondering why had God left me. My sponsor hadn't given up on me. He came to visit and we talked about everything. He said, "It's not the end of the world, use the time as a lesson and get to know God." At the time I felt like punching him out, because to me it was the end of the world. You can imagine a 240 pound, six-foot bearded slob sitting with his head in his hands and crying like a little child. But little did I know that this wasn't the end, it was the beginning.

When I got back to my cell I got on my knees and cried out to God to help me and just as I got off my knees an officer came in and said we could use the library. I borrowed the Big Book and started to read it, every part of it. I kept in touch with my sponsor and he sent me some other books to read. I feel from then on the compulsion was taken away, when I honestly asked God for help.

I truly believe that a day at a time and as long as I work the Twelve Steps of recovery, I need not drink ever again and I don't want to. I believe that the Program has turned my life around, and my Higher Power has slowly brought me back to sanity. I can't be grateful enough. I now have the love of my family back and I am as happy as I allow myself to be. I have also been getting one meeting a week in here; the members of an outside meeting have so patiently come in and shared. I owe a lot to them and to my sponsor. The Program works, even on me, and I love it.

110. PARTY GIRL

I was very active socially when I was using. By that, I mean I spent a lot of time in the various nightspots around town, enough to become known as a party girl. I was always getting in the car with my girlfriend on any given night (it didn't matter if it was a work night), going to some bar or some party or SOMEWHERE, looking for action, looking for men, looking for excitement, always feeling restless, bitchy, and empty. Whether I was happy or unhappy, I was always looking for something "more." Too much was never enough. Maybe at first, for a couple of days or weeks, but eventually it got old or boring, and I felt let down. So I'd go on hopelessly looking for something "more."

I've found it very difficult at times to break out of this old pattern of thinking in recovery. Turning my will and life over to the care of my Higher Power day by day is not always easy, and I still have a fear that my Higher Power will not give me the things I think I need to be happy. I feel this fear and distrust particularly when I am going through spells of loneliness, depression, or self-pity.

I don't have a single magical answer which has helped me. But I have learned these things since coming to the Program: On my own I am nothing. I need my Higher Power; I need willingness and action on my part by working the Steps; and I need hope that my fear will be removed. God's will, not mine.

I know my Higher Power has kept me abstinent for a while now and worked a lot of cleansing and healing in me. I've seen God do the same for so many people. I know the answer lies with my Higher Power and the Fellowship. I know that when I've gotten off my butt and helped others through service work, I'M OKAY. I know that going to meetings regularly and sharing my real feelings makes me feel OKAY. I know that when I work the Steps I feel OKAY. I know that if I keep on praying and surrendering these old ideas I will continue to be OKAY.

Then maybe I'll suddenly realize that God has done for me what I could not do for myself, and thank Him.

111. AUTHORITY FIGURES

Being young and in the Program isn't always easy. Although we are young, we had many very adult experiences and adult pain in our using days. A lot of this was caused by our mixed-up thinking and feelings when dealing with parents, teachers, police—you know, "authority figures."

When we were using, we constantly fought any and all authority figures. No one could tell us what to do or when to do it. No one knew what was good for us or what we needed. Our drugs of choice were our authority. Our addiction told us what to do and when to do it, what was good for us and what we needed.

We never liked rules or being told what to do. The rules were broken and if an authority figure, especially Mom or Dad, said no, we said yes.

These rebellious acts can become dangerous in our recovery. We must realize that we **don't** always know what's good for us. Our previous experiences have proven that. We must begin to understand that these older people, these authority figures, have been around awhile. They have been through some of the things we've been through and they have been where we are headed. Controlling our own lives got us nowhere before recovery. Let's give these people a chance without fighting them on every rule or suggestion they offer. I've found out it's important to remain teachable in recovery.

Who knows? We may be surprised what we can learn if we listen and accept rather than argue, criticize, or rebel.

112. FROM MANIPULATING TO LISTENING

Even as a small child (4 or 5 years old), I can remember manipulating parents and friends with my cuteness and smooth talk. The older I got, the better I got at manipulation and being a con artist. The better I got, the more I got—booze, cocaine, money, cars. I could lie and cheat people without guilt. I could look my parents in the eye and lie straight to their faces. I got so good I began to believe my own lies.

I got everything I wanted when I wanted it. By the time I walked through the doors of the Fellowship, my manipulations and lies had caught up with me. I *was* feeling guilt, and it was hard for me to look anyone in the eyes and say anything at all.

But I still wanted everything *now*. I wanted what everyone else had, but I didn't want to work for it. I wanted it *given* to me, like everything else in my life. I didn't know how to honestly work for something and actually earn it. This was something totally new to me.

This "one day at a time" business just wasn't working. I'd talk at every meeting and thought I sounded good. I thought I had all the answers. I thought I was working so hard and was getting nothing in return. I wasn't getting "what everyone else had." Once again, I was faking it. Then someone told me, "take the cotton out of your ears and put it in your mouth," which was a nice way of telling me to shut up! They went on and let me know a few things that have helped me. I can't con or manipulate the Program. I can't "talk the talk" and not "walk the walk." I can't expect to be given the benefits of recovery unless I work for them—that's right, work for them to the best of my ability.

It's been six months now since I was told to shut up, and I've been listening. I'm becoming a good listener. When I listen to what wiser and more experienced members say, I grow in the Program.

113. FLIRTING

I'm a young woman with four years of recovery. I've always known how to "swing a hip" and "bat an eyelash" and use it to my advantage. If you've got it, flaunt it, right? Well, I did.

When I was using, it got me into trouble. My flirting wasn't always intentional. A lot of times it was just me being me—part of my personality. Then I began to see how I affected people and started using it to my advantage. I was good. I always got along better with men than with women. I never had *any* female friends. They were either full of jealousy or they just hung around because I knew the "cool" people and where to get the best coke.

During my first days in treatment, I got really bugged because three guys kept hitting on me. I couldn't understand why they were bothering me. I was tuning down my body talk and keeping to myself. I didn't want to get involved. When I got

out and began going to meetings, I would get dirty
looks from a few of the female members. I'd get the
stares and drools from the guys like I was a bitch in
heat. Once again, it bothered me. I wanted recovery, not more promiscuity. I felt branded.

Trying to control my "body talk" has become
a big part of my recovery. I'm not responsible for
the way I look, but I've learned in recovery that I *am*
responsible for the way I present myself to others.
I've learned how to become friends with other
women. My sponsor and my new female friends
have shown me a lot about how I was flirting when
I didn't think I was. I now know the difference
between flirting and being sociable.

I'd been looking at the problem (men hitting
on me) from the wrong direction. I didn't want to
give up the real or imagined control and power-
tripping my flirting got me. I see now how my
flirting makes my life unmanageable, just like my
active addiction did. I've learned about humility
also, and am much less conceited and self-centered
about how I look.

114. SLEEPING AROUND

Relationships came and went in my "using"
days and a few have come and gone in my "sober

days." It's sometimes tough being young, single, and vulnerable in recovery because it seems there are many other people in the same boat. There are quite a few people looking for that special someone. When we start looking for that special someone in our recovery, we begin to find out it's not easy.

When I was using, there were no strings attached. There really was no such thing as a relationship. I had been a victim of a violent rape when I was seventeen and from that point on until I sobered up at 20 not much mattered. I felt as if I had been used and betrayed.

This brought about a lot of sleeping around, doing whatever felt good. Having sex then was always under the influence. I was just going through the motions. It didn't matter what their last name was or if they had been in prison or had a job. It was all part of my misery, pain, and suffering. Any time someone came along who wanted to get close to me and really loved me, I'd shut them out. Not only members of the opposite sex, but my family, too.

I destroyed a lot of relationships in a very short period of time. I did that in early recovery, too. I met people who wanted to spend time with me right out of treatment. It usually turned out they wanted to "change me" or control my life and my Program. So I'd end it.

I'd go to a meeting and be hounded. It was almost like I had to either be very cruel or hide in a corner. I didn't like that. It's been hard to be truthful and just say I'm not interested for fear of hurting someone again.

Once I began recovery, I realized my emotions were pretty screwed up. There was a lot of deep pain in me. The Program asks us to deal with that pain and get those skeletons out of the closet. This hasn't been easy for me. There were too many skeletons I chose to forget. The thought of those skeletons literally made me sick to my stomach. I finally got around to doing my Fourth Step and got rid of a lot of that garbage. I have talked with a counselor and my sponsor about the rape, and have gotten help.

One of the gifts of recovery for me has been getting rid of the pain from the past, gaining forgiveness for myself and others, and taking away that constant pressure I've put on myself about finding that special someone. Recovery *has* given me a new relationship, a special someone—recovery has given *me* back to me.

115. HAVING BEEN ABUSED

When many of us began our recovery and our bodies start getting rid of all those chemicals, we started to experience emotions from our childhood that need to be dealt with. Entering the Program as young adults is a good beginning. These bad experiences haven't had as much time to cause the damage they could if we waited ten or twenty years more before dealing with them.

Bad experiences are quite common with young addicts/alcoholics. Those experiences could be incest, child molestation, rape, physical abuse by parents or others, neglect, divorce, single-parent families, or no parents at all. These examples can all cause severe emotional damage if they aren't dealt with. They can also halt our progress. We begin to feel as if we're on a dead-end street with no way out.

These events could very well have triggered our substance abuse. It may have seemed an easier way of dealing with it—staying high and/or drunk so we didn't have to face it, feel it, or deal with it.

We have learned in recovery how to ask for help. If we have to get help with these negative experiences, we can do that. Some of us get help from professional counselors. These events don't need to be our excuse for relapse.

116. FLASHBACKS AND NIGHTMARES

There will always be something that will remind us of our past—both good and bad—usually bad. It may come to us as a flashback or daydream, sometimes nightmares. They are triggered by many things. Maybe the smell of a freshly lit match will remind us of smoking coke, or the sound of birds chirping early in the morning will remind us of that sick feeling of trying to sleep while our heart is pounding out of our chest and we're begging God to just let us sleep. It may be a song on the radio that will remind us of a past relationship we screwed up or ended in tragedy. It may be a movie that reminds us of the violence and pain that we kept in our lives. It may be when we read in the local news of a friend or even a stranger dying of a drug overdose or a drug-related crime.

These are just a few examples of "things" that could trigger these memories. These feelings can be both helpful and harmful. They can be helpful when we deal with the situation by accepting it, forgiving ourselves, and turning it over to our

Higher Power—maybe even share our feelings with a friend, sponsor, or at a meeting. They can be harmful if we dwell on the guilt, anger, and negative feelings. When we lock this up inside, we turn into walking time bombs ready to explode. When we do finally explode, although it may be only weeks or even months or years before it happens, it usually leads to relapse.

117. BOUNDARIES

We didn't care about boundaries or limits when we were using. No one could set any fences around us—we'd cross them. There were no steps or traditions in the old days, no one we would listen to.

Boundaries are a very important part of everyone's recovery. They can help us grow as individuals and better ourselves and they can prevent relapse.

Many of us come from alcoholic families and/or broken homes—that's pretty common. A lot of us had no discipline. We all learned from what our guardians showed us. Some of that was pretty unhealthy. We were learning from other's examples and basing our boundaries on that. By the time we reach the doors of the Fellowship our minds are pretty warped. There isn't much we know about what is right or wrong for us. This becomes very critical in our recovery. We have to start fresh like a newborn baby. It doesn't matter how old we are or how long we used, by the time we get here everyone needs to start over and learn what's right or wrong for themselves.

A good way of doing this is by taking a look—honestly—at our past behaviors and where our actions led us. Some examples would be running away from home, not going to school, disrespecting your parents and other people, and so on. All these things led us deeper into our addictions.

We will need to know when we're headed back in that direction. Until we can learn what we are capable of and what we need to stay away from, and until we can truly get honest with ourselves and find the boundaries that best suit us, we need to use the Twelve Steps and Traditions, our slogans, our sponsors, our meetings, and listen to what the old-timers have to say. Let them set our boundaries for us until we're able to set our own. Let's "not drink or drug and go to meetings," let's "let go and let God," let's do it "one day at a time," let's "keep it simple," let's "not quit five minutes before the miracle."

Let us use these simple suggestions as our boundaries and live our new life by them. There are no guarantees in this Program but I can guarantee if we live by these suggestions and make them work for us our chances are pretty good for a much better life in recovery.

118. THINGS TO REMEMBER; THINGS TO FORGET

As a recovering young person, what can I expect to
    find?
Some hills, some valleys, some mountains to climb.
A lot to be learned and a lot to forget,
And a mind not as smart as I thought it was yet.
I'll try to forget my very first drink,
How important it made me feel and think;
I'll try to forget the short period of fun,
When I thought I was greater than anyone,
When false courage made me reckless and bold
And I was convinced I would never grow old.
I'll try to remember how sick I've been,
And remember each day to thank God again.

I'll remember the headaches, the heartaches, and
    shame,
The remorse, the guilt, the loneliness, and pain.
I'll remember all the misery brought on by one
    drink.
I'll remember I'm an alcoholic and I must learn to
    think.
I'll forget the first drink and remember the last
To find a future better than my past.
I'll remember the most important time is "today."
I'll live and let live and thank God for A.A.

119. A SELFISH PROGRAM

Let's always remember what came first in our
lives when we were using. It's easy: it was our
addiction. It wasn't our job, family, car, friends,
school—it wasn't anything except our addiction. It
had 100% control over us.

If we want what "they've got," then we must
learn to put our recovery *first* to make it *last*. We
become the most important person in our life. It
sounds selfish, but it's a very selfish Program.
After all, how can we really take care of someone
else when we can't even take care of ourselves? Oh,
we knew how to be selfish when we were using,

when it came down to the last beer in the fridge or hit in the pipe. We were selfish when we only had one fix, one joint, one beer, or one rock left. We were selfish when the stash was gone and we needed more. We knew how to be selfish, all right. Now we need to learn to be concerned about ourselves and our recovery. We need to take care of ourselves first.

120. IN THE MIDDLE OF A MIRACLE

For some reason, I just started thinking about my first year in sobriety and remembering details more clearly than I was previously able to. I am coming up on my twenty-first birthday and my sixth A.A. birthday.

Yes, I sobered up at age fifteen, and if you're wondering when I started drinking, it was when I was eleven. Of course, I'm an addict also, so that helped get me to A.A. a lot faster.

My drinking story is not much different from yours except that alcohol wasn't as easy for me to get, so I made sure that I ran with people who *could* get it. We drank whatever and used whatever, to get as loaded as we possibly could. My drunks were fairly protected because my "friends" watched out for me, so I didn't go to jail or a hospital, but I now know that was only through God's grace. And, of course, I was still living at home, so I didn't have to fend for myself while I was drinking. If I had I surely would've been a goner.

Even with all this confusion in my head, the part of my story that gets really strange is my first year of *sobriety*.

My first sponsor was a "ninety-seven-pound weakling." I remember first "wanting what she had" after seeing her at an A.A. dance. At the time I was only a couple of months sober. She was young, she was a good dancer (I was too), and I watched her. She was also very thin, and having always been overweight enough to bother me, I was envious of her size.

I guess I didn't meet or speak to her until a couple of months later (in those days I wasn't apt to just saunter up and introduce myself—I was very hostile). But when I heard her talk in a meeting, I found she was a year younger than I and had six months more sobriety. I don't remember officially meeting her or asking her to sponsor me, but we soon became close. We were to spend almost every weekend night of the following several months at late meetings, coffee afterward, and then all-night rap sessions. I needed that because I was unable to tell anyone how different I felt. I saw all these sober people with years in the Program, and my insides just didn't match their outsides, and I was too self-willed to ask anyone for direction of any kind, especially involving the Steps.

At any rate, when I was eleven months sober and had left my mother's home the month before and moved into my sponsor's previous residence— a $40-a-month single garage with a bathroom next door by the neighbor's pool—I was in the definite process of a nervous breakdown. She came to see me and told me to do the Third Step with her. I told her to get out of my house, and what did she mean by do the Step *with* her? You see, in my insanity, I thought the book said not to do the Step with anyone, lest they might misunderstand. How she must have chuckled at this. Well, that night, we did the Third Step together on our knees and shortly thereafter I came out of the breakdown and headed for my first A.A. birthday.

The specialness of my first year, with all my insanity and the patience my sponsor showed me, I shall be grateful for forever. Had I not been able to develop a foundation in sobriety through her friendship, I might never have made it this far.

And I leave you with this: If you ever think you are overdue for a miracle in your life, just remember you're right in the middle of one.

121. SPIRITUALITY

To a lot of us the word "God" was one word we didn't want to hear, maybe because of guilt, fear, or anger (resentment), or just a lack of understanding about spirituality.

The first of the Twelve Steps suggests that "we admit we are powerless and our lives have become unmanageable." We then come "to believe in a Power greater than ourselves," then make "a decision to turn our will and our lives over to God *as we understood him.*" Each individual sees his or her own Higher Power through their own eyes. It may be Jesus Christ, Buddha, Mohammed, the Fellowship, or nature. For many of us, just being able to be here at this moment to read this book proves that there is definitely a Higher Power working in our lives. Because with just "ourselves," we are very destructive and dangerous.

Spirituality isn't something you just ask for and it's given—it's something you have to look for and you will find it. In time, every one of us will find a God of our understanding. It's something that is progressive, not perfect. When we tried to do everything without "God," we now see where that took us. Without opening our hearts and our minds to this idea our efforts will seem meaningless.

122. RESULTS, NOT ALWAYS PROMISES

When I first heard at meetings and read in my *Big Book* "The Promises," I was blown away by the wonderful picture of a life of serenity which would unfold for me. I had, of course, much to learn.

What I had done was to take them totally out of context, viewing them as a package of goodies which would somehow drop into my lap as long as I stayed sober. Fortunately, I had a good sponsor, so I had made an early start on the Twelve Steps. I came to realize that these were not promises which were going to be delivered by others. Their placing on pages 83 and 84 of the *Big Book* comes at the end of a 26-page discussion of working the first nine Steps. The Promises would begin to arrive in my life by me being honest and willing in working through of the first nine Steps. In other words, they were to be results rather than promises.

I came into the Program at the age of eighteen and just had my fifth anniversary. The results have been a much better life, by working all the Steps. Now I know the Promises are results I must continue to work for, one day at a time.

There are many other promises throughout the text of the Big Book which are examples of what we can and will have if we thoroughly follow the path. I leave you with one about hanging in there—"If you persist, remarkable things will happen."

123. SHOULDN'T IT BE EASIER THAN THIS?

It's been hard for me to accept that recovery is about progress, not perfection. I've been in the Program almost two years now and am still having my share of bad days. Hey, shouldn't it be easier than this?

I came into the Program thinking if I stopped using, things would be 100% better. I still think that way sometimes—all or nothing, black or white, yes or no. I try to remember to quit looking for the magic. Today, my life is much simpler. My days of doubting whether recovery is worth it are fewer. Sobriety was just the first step; changing my life and how I deal with others and myself has been the hard part.

I have a job I like. I have real friends and I'm active in the Program. This type of life agrees with me. But when I'm by myself too much, get into self-pity, and again think all or nothing, I get really stuck. They say "an addict alone is in bad company." When I'm like this I think, "What's the use?" I back myself into a corner of self-obsession and think there's no way out. I think I can't stand life's problems any more, but then this Program provides an answer and the bad times pass. I'm learning how to live with myself.

Before I came into the Program I really had no freedom. I didn't understand the word. The only meaning it had for me was the idea of being released from prison or being able to fly. I like both those ideas, but the only things that gave me the illusion of freedom were alcohol and drugs. It never lasted because something always went bad when I was wasted. I was in prison, the prisoner of active addiction without knowing it.

I knew I was miserable, but I didn't know why. I thought I was under a curse and felt cut off from the rest of the human race. I was in a trap and desperate to get out. That meant I was at the mercy of other people's whims, and only knew how to be what I thought other people wanted me to be. I was always being blown around by the winds of circumstance.

The very first experience with freedom ever in my life was when someone said to me, "Do you want to stop drinking and drugging?" and I said, "Yes," realizing that I really meant it. The second experience was when someone said to me, "You need never get wasted again." Both these ideas had never before reached my brain and it was the first glimpse of reality and sanity for a really sick and desperate person.

The longer I stay in recovery, the more I learn about freedom. "Shouldn't it be easier than this?" is about freedom. The freedom to stay stuck, "awfulizing," or facing stinking thinking and bad times head on. Knowing is not enough; I must apply. Being willing is not enough; I must do.

124. ALL OR NOTHING

All my life, everything was a question of "all or nothing"—job, school, relationships, possessions, obsessions, living, loving, and above all, drinking and drugging. No half-measures: totally wasted or white-knuckled abstinence. No half-pleasures: overworking or burnout. No half-treasures: money and security or broke and homeless.

If I couldn't win, I lost by giving up. Fight or flight. Victory or defeat. No surrender. No middle road. Just sad, bad, mad extremes.

So here is another paradox of the Program: As with my former life, so my new life in recovery must also be all or nothing. But this time it is positive, absolute abstinence from my addiction one day at a time—or death for all days. Today, the giving of my attitudes and will to my Higher Power and the principles of the Program must be all-out and complete.

If I am half-hearted about this, I may not be using today, but I'll be stuck and going nowhere. If I put all my energy into recovery, then—and here's the rub—everything else in my life today takes on the non-excessive, non-obsessive and non-depressive blessing of balance that some call serenity.

125. IN OR AROUND THE PROGRAM

Some of us come into the Program to satisfy our parents or someone else. Others come into the

Program on their own. Some of us do what is suggested and others just kind of hang out and talk the talk, but don't walk the walk. Sometimes we may feel we really want this thing called "serenity" but we feel something is missing. We may even want to start helping others find their way. Before we can do this, we need to ask ourselves: are we just "around the Program" or are we "in the Program"? We may catch ourselves saying, "I'm in the Program," but are we really doing what is necessary to maintain healthy sobriety?

Do you find yourself only using the Program in an emergency? Do you only practice the principles and Steps when something comes up? Are you missed if you don't show up at a meeting? Do you stick around afterwards and mingle? The answers to these questions will help us understand if we are just "around" or actually in the Program.

If we don't get "in" the Program, we can't offer help to others. We can't give away what we don't have!

126. PICK UP THE PHONE

A year sober and still having coke dreams . . . does that sound familiar? Upon entering the Program, some of us still have a strong desire for our drug of choice. Some of us have no desire at all. Like everything else about this Program, it's different for everyone. There is no right or wrong answer for the reasoning behind it, but for those of us who have that desire, craving, or temptation, there are options we have to use before giving in to that monkey on our backs.

One of the easiest and most helpful is "phone therapy." So many of us let our addictions take back control and we end up in the streets again. *Then*, we call our sponsor and come back into the Program after however long it takes to come back. All of that additional pain and suffering can be prevented by picking up the phone *before* we pick up that next drink or drug. A call can be made to a sponsor, family member, friend, fellow member, or hotline. It doesn't matter who you call, but it's important that you call. After all, it's that next drink that could be your last. So pick up the phone before you pick up your next drink or drug, not after. It may be too late then. One phone call could save your life. Help is only a phone call away.

127. WILLINGNESS

None of us as alcoholics and/or addicts have to go back to the life we used to live—if you want to call it living. We have choices in our lives and no one can take that away from us. The key to our new lives is willingness.

Willingness will help us to accept our disease and responsibilities. Willingness gives us that extra "strength" to change our behaviors and attitudes. Willingness allows us to keep an open mind about our spirituality. With willingness, we must include actions, growing and learning.

Willingness is the key.

128. IDENTIFY, DON'T COMPARE

We all have our different stories of how long we used, what we used, and what happened when we used it. We all have our own experiences, beliefs, and ways of living. This is why it's so very important that we don't compare our Program with someone else's. Although we all have our disease in common, and a lot of our stories are similar, many of us work the Program the way the Program works best for us.

The Program offers us simple Steps and Traditions that we use as tools to recovery. They suggest everyone have a sponsor. They suggest we go to meetings. The *Big Book* speaks of a Power greater than ourselves. Each of these are interpreted as each person understands it. It's not the same for everyone. Some don't believe in God. Others don't have "a sponsor"; they may use their home group as a sponsor. Some only go to one meeting a month. Others may go every day. Some may be able to hang out with friends who have a drink every now and then. Others can't be around it at all. Some live by the *Big Book* and can quote verses from it. Some live by the Bible. Some speak at meetings; others don't. Some have lives outside the Fellowship Halls; others have no life but within the Fellowship.

The point is, when we come into this Program, we are all different, and we will see things differently from others. We must try to remember to "take what we can use and leave the rest" and work the Program that works the best for us, to the best of our ability. Do what works best for you.

129. CHANGE IS A PROCESS

Over an indefinite period of time, we are all asked to make a lot of changes in our lives when we begin our recovery. Those changes will take time. They're an ongoing process which won't happen overnight. We won't see a bolt of lightning come down and strike us, changing us, making us all better.

None of us have it all together, and there's nothing wrong with admitting that. Sometimes we may need to take time out to work on ourselves. We may not have much to say at a meeting. Every positive change we make in our recovery makes us a better person. Some of us may ask what it is exactly that we need to change. I was told that I needed to change "everything I say, everything I think, and everything I do." That was overwhelming, but I knew it was true. I began to realize and accept that change meant growth.

Change in recovery isn't so difficult. It's our resistance to it that makes it difficult. "Change is a process, not an event."

130. GROWING UP

Growing up is a very slow process, and a very difficult one for me. I don't know about anyone else, but when I got here I thought I *was* grown up. I found out I was an adult in body, but a child in everything else.

I came to the Program when I was 21 years old. Even though I was a shell of a human being when I got here, I still thought of myself as an adult.

Over the past three years I've come to know the child in me (or maybe I should say the baby!). In a lot of ways, I am a child in an adult's body. On some days this can be very uncomfortable.

Growth can be a painful thing for someone like me, who thought they knew everything. I am adult enough today to admit that I have a long way to go. But thanks to this Program and the tools I have learned here, I know I am growing in the right direction.

I may have the emotions of a 12-year-old today, but that's an improvement over the 2-year-old I was when I got here. I have grown a lot in the past three years. I no longer throw temper tantrums. I no longer sit in the middle of the floor curled up in the fetal position and cry. I'm no longer so selfish and self-centered that the only person I can think about is me.

I am not the overgrown child I used to be, thanks to this Program. The 12 Steps are teaching me how to grow up. I am beginning to fit this body. I hope the future holds more growth for me, because that's what recovery is all about. This is not a maintenance program, it's a growth program. In order to grow I must take some action.

131. SECRETS

When beginning our recovery, many of us come into this Program with nightmares of our past and many character defects. Remaining abstinent from drugs and alcohol can be pretty easy. It's dealing with our secrets of the past that become more difficult. It can be very painful at times. The guilt, anger, and resentments can be overwhelming. We find ourselves saying, "I can't deal with it. It hurts too much. I can't." Before you say "I can't," say "I'll try." It's definitely worth the effort. Each nightmare shared and worked out is another battle won. It's another weight lifted off our shoulders. It makes all the other nightmares just a little easier to deal with.

Try to remember, we're only as sick as our secrets.

132. I WAS N.U.T.S.

I got through treatment and got my six-month medallion. Things were O.K. During my seventh month, I really hit a brick wall and felt like using again. I've gotten through that period when I was N.U.T.S. You know, "Not Using The Steps." All I had been doing was being a Two-Stepper. I wasn't using (Step 1); I was going to a lot of meetings; and I was carrying the message (Step 12). I've found out now I'd better learn what the message is first, by working all 12 Steps.

Most of us are used to eating our desserts before dinner is over. We celebrate before we've won. We assume the outcome before the event. The problem with this type of behavior is it takes no account of reality. Things move from beginning to end. The alphabet reads from A to Z. This seems so simple, but it can be tricky for people like you and me who are used to taking shortcuts.

My sponsor has helped me change from being a Two-Stepper to working all the Steps. I had the same sponsor during my first six months and during my seventh month crisis. There's a difference now, because I call my sponsor. Before I just said I had a sponsor, but didn't call him. It's important I put all my effort into every Step. If I do, the outcome will take care of itself. Just like the slogan says, "We are responsible for the effort, not the outcome."

My sponsor told me to read "No Free Ride" in my daily meditation book, *Easy Does It*. I'd like to share it with you:

NO FREE RIDE

The elevator is broken; use the Steps. —Anonymous

"Elevators are easy. We push a button and we go right to the top. The way is fast, quick, and silent. We don't work up a sweat. We don't get out of breath. We can't trip and fall. There is not much time to communicate with anyone else along the way so we don't have to use any effort or thought. We can daydream as we face the front of the car and stare at the numbers as they change from floor to floor.

Then the elevator breaks and we crash to the ground. Those of us who survive are told to take the Steps to get where we want to go. Our addictions were our elevators out of living. The chemical highs we experienced were just like an elevator ride. Until we crashed.

I will sometimes sweat, stumble, get out of breath in my climb, but I'll take the time to talk with and learn from others who are taking the Steps with me."

133. POWERLESS

After a few failed attempts at recovery, I finally understood that the First Step said nothing about admitting that I was an alcoholic; it called upon me to admit that I was "powerless over alcohol" and that my life "had become unmanageable." The idea that I was an alcoholic wasn't the surrender that the First Step talks about. I could have admitted my alcoholism from then to doomsday, but until I admitted that alcohol was my master, there was little or no hope for recovery. When I finally took the First Step and threw in the towel, I was on my way. It took complete surrender to bring victory.

After the First Step, I found I needed another power greater than myself to keep me sober. I went on to the Second and Third Steps without second thoughts, and the strength came. A Higher Power had always been there, just waiting for me to ask for help, and when I did, it was not wanting. The insanity of drinking fell away. When my Higher Power took over my will and the management of my life, I began to find a peace and stability I'd never known.

As I've moved up the ladder of sanity (the Twelve Steps), I have gained more peace of mind. The ups and downs of life don't shake me, and I have been able to handle several tragic incidents without relapsing.

But my alcoholic self is not dead—he's just in limbo, waiting for complacency or stinking thinking to open the door for his reentry into my life. That I must never forget. I am an alcoholic and powerless over alcohol. There are some musts for me: I must make meetings; I must have faith in the God of my understanding; I must work the principles of the Program each and every day in all my affairs; I must never take that first drink; and I must love my neighbor as myself.

Also, I must never forget the craziness of my life before I surrendered to my master—alcohol. Others may say there are no musts in the Program. That's their privilege. But for me, those musts are very important.

My alcoholic self will live as long as I; whether we ever get back together is up to me. With the help of my Higher Power and the wonderful people who make up the Fellowship, that other self and I will not meet again.

134. INVENTORIES

Admitting I was an alcoholic and that I could be wrong was something I found very hard, prior to AA finding me and allowing me to find myself.

In my simple mind I always find Step Ten tied up with Step Four. Like different lenses on a camera, both do the same thing while giving a different viewpoint. Step Ten for me is taken within the context of the whole Program. Otherwise, it's like a car without an engine.

During my first months in recovery, I was forever denying my faults, refusing to accept that I was wrong, or that I was capable of doing, or had done the things I heard others openly admit doing. Honesty certainly was not part of my life in those early days. Then came "The Steps." Yes, it was painful having to look at myself in a way I had never done before. Many times I cried, many times I lied; I refused to accept the truths that were confronting me at every meeting. Nonetheless, something kept bringing me back; week in, week out, I would get to a meeting. Each one made me grow a little, each piece of knowledge forced me to look at myself, to question all previous values, to re-assess, to look at where I had been, where I was, and where I wanted to go. Yes, it was painful, and I cried. I cried inside and out, and it hurt.

Many times I have tried to explain to people what the Program has given me—in the end I always come back to the same thing—freedom.

Strange that I had to be in the prison of active addiction to find the real freedom that was so much lacking in my life prior to my coming in. Step Ten is a constant reminder to me, that all the pain, all the suffering and craziness, is just around the corner waiting for me—if I want it. It reminds me of what I have today spiritually, physically, and materially. It is a constant reminder to me that I must not allow myself to become complacent.

Being wrong at times seems to be part of being human. That's easy enough to accept. My mistakes now don't seem like the disasters I used to imagine them to be. Today Step Ten allows me to reflect on my mistakes and grow from them as a result, and occasionally, to laugh at some of them.

But this Step is not just about looking at our faults, our mistakes, etc. It is about recognizing our assets, acknowledging being right, being aware of our good points. It is this aspect of Step Ten that gives each of us continual growth within the Fellowship as well as in our day-to-day lives.

Each meeting I attend *is* a Step Ten for it takes me back to roots, reminding me of my first introduction to the Program. With every talk that someone gives, I continue to take personal inventory.

Step Ten is a pause along the way on the road

to recovery to look at my progress, my growth. It allows me to see any detour I make from the Program. It reminds me to get the full benefits of the Tenth Step, and removes the fear of admitting I was wrong.

Step Ten emphasizes the importance of the continuous nature of the Program. It illustrates that this Program is a way of life, something which needs to be applied to day-to-day living, not just a Program that has importance only during meetings. What one does *between* meetings is as important as what one does during meetings.

Like Step Four, Step Ten requires honesty, otherwise it has no meaning and serves no purpose. Honesty demands seeing one's faults, admitting one is wrong when necessary, recognizing that one's judgments can be wrong, that one's viewpoint of events can also be wrong. It tells me I must accept the things I cannot change and change the things I can.

The Tenth Step is my buffer against getting stuck and complacent. It tells me: "I am responsible . . . when anyone, anywhere reaches out for help . . . ." For, had no one been there when I needed it most, it is unlikely I would be here today to share these thoughts.

135. PARTYING AND HOLIDAYS

No more parties. No more dancing. No more fun. These were my thoughts when I first started the Program. I had the P.L.O.M.s ("**P**oor **L**ittle **O**ld **M**e's") for quite a while. If I wasn't going to be getting loaded, I figured I wasn't going to be going to parties, dancing, or having fun, because I was always loaded when I did these things.

I wasn't the first one or the last one to begin recovery wondering how I was going to handle parties and holidays without alcohol or drugs. I try to remember that keeping it simple also means first things first, so I have to try to be as honest with myself as possible when I ask myself the question, "Is recovery the most important thing in my life?" If so, then nothing is more important than staying away from slippery people, places, and playthings.

We are reminded by our sponsors and fellow members that we need a very good reason before we attend what might be a stressful situation that may test our recovery. Once I thought that other people at parties might make it difficult for me. Today I know only I can make it difficult for myself.

The very best answer I can give myself, if I think a party might be too much for me to handle, is don't go. There are many things to do in recovery that are enjoyable, and not stressful. I've put together the following list which has helped me with holidays and parties:

    1.   Not to go to a party or out dancing if I feel it's not safe for me to do so.

    2.   Ask my fellow members and sponsor for advice on going to parties.

    3.   Take a Program friend with me.

    4.   Keep a list of phone numbers of recovery friends with me. Even if I don't use them, it's a comfort to know they are in my pocket.

    5.   Am I going for the right reasons, such as to meet new people and friends and have a good time? Or am I trying to get back to that old using atmosphere and those old thinking habits?

136. SPONSORING

    As a young person myself, I think one of the greatest feelings I've ever experienced was when another young person came up to me after a meeting and asked me if I would be their sponsor. Sponsoring has been one of the biggest contributions to my recovery today. I think I've actually learned more from my sponsee than I've taught. Sponsoring, in my opinion, is more like being a friend when a friend is needed. It's not giving advice; it's sharing experiences. It's not telling the sponsee what to do; it's guiding him/her in the right direction, towards the ways of the Program. We can guide; we can teach. There will come a time when our work will be passed on and our sponsee will also become a sponsor.

137. GOING HOME

Coming out of treatment back into society can be a very scary experience. The drugs and alcohol are always going to be there. They will always be readily available. How do we deal with that? One of the hardest things about "going home" is dealing with our peer groups, our "friends" at school. Where do we tell them we've been? How do we deal with being sociable again without the drug/alcohol parties? What do we do when we're walking down the hallways in between classes and somebody calls us a slut, alcoholic, druggie, "big time user," or a skank? We can't just drop out, give up, or run and hide. That's what we did in our using days. We somehow need to deal with the cards that are being dealt and play out our hand.

Here are a few suggestions that may be help-ful. First of all, we need to believe in ourselves and in our Program. Believe in a Power greater than ourselves. Some sort of spiritual program is very important. Remember our support groups, the friends we met in treatment who are going through the same daily trials and tribulations that we are. Try to accept the fact that a lot of our peers have never been where we were and can't understand where we're headed. It's a kind of ignorance on their part. They don't understand. Someday they might, but it's not our problem. Remember our old behaviors and how we may have lashed out with anger or returned the name-calling, and how that never got us anywhere.

138. I DON'T GET IT

I've been in recovery six months now, and I really don't understand that much about the Pro-gram. But I can say, I have more faith now than when I came in. I think one of the first things I said to my sponsor was, "I don't get it." I didn't understand what recovery was going to help me with, except not using. Who or what to believe? My old friends and ways of doing things? I was still full of myself and starved for any meaning in my life.

When I said to my sponsor, "I don't get it," he answered, "Why do you have to? If you don't understand why the sky is blue, does that make the sky a different color? Just because you don't understand what recovery is all about, does that make the Program less helpful?"

I was looking for proof and have found out that I need to just believe and to trust. Step Two asked me for faith, to accept that the Program works without instant proof, and to be able to ask my Higher Power for help with my problems. I began to use my Higher Power before I really understood it.

For instance, when I hear stories from those who decide to "go out" and try using again, I don't have to follow their example in order to prove them right or wrong. I can trust their experience. The only proof I need that the Program works is to look to my sponsor and all the other members, and listen to their stories of how it was and how it is now. Faith in the power of the Steps reminds me that one of them begins, "Came to believe . . . ." Unless I stick to my belief and faith in the Steps, I am in danger of maybe relapsing or staying stuck, wondering why the sky is blue.

139. PUSHING BUTTONS

Our family, parents, and loved ones can "push our buttons," and some say, that's because they installed them.

Many of us grew up filled with shame, and it has continued into our later lives. Addiction and shame go together. We were told we could do better in school. We were told we weren't living up to our potential. We learned there was *something* wrong with us. We *should* do better. Guilt is when we make a mistake; shame is when we believe we *are* a mistake.

Our recovery allows us to identify and work out of our shame-filled past. We can't force the people in our lives who push our buttons to change. We *can* change our attitudes and the way we react to button-pushers and the old unmanageable tapes in our heads. Not being perfect no longer means not being worthwhile.

Today, we're learning not to let the button-pushers affect our outlook. Our sponsor and friends are always there to make sure our button-pushers have much less power over us.

140. ATTITUDE OF GRATITUDE

When I first came into this Program and heard those words at the beginning of a meeting, it made me sick to my stomach. I had nothing, at that time, to be grateful for. The last thing I wanted to hear was that mushy crap about gratitude and how good everyone felt and how grateful they were.

At the time I was full of anger, fear, resentment, guilt, and confusion. I had no idea what gratitude was or how to get it. I kept on going to the meetings, kept on listening, and kept on keeping my mouth shut. I eventually started to see what these people were talking about.

I had been dwelling only on the negative, rather than finding the positive. I was only looking at what I *didn't* have, rather than being grateful for what I *did* have. In order for me to be grateful, there were a few things I needed to do, and I found myself doing them on a daily basis. First I had to simply stop what I was doing and think. I share with my Higher Power and turn over my ungrateful feelings. I take a look at my past (go back over my First Step), then look at where I am now and where I'm heading—without future tripping, of course. Then I think about how much better I feel, both physically and mentally. I accept that I need to forgive myself and become more humble, and that I must live in the present.

Then I can become grateful. I can be grateful to my Higher Power for watching over me and guiding me. I can be grateful for my recovery—my new life. I can be grateful for the support of my family and friends. I can be grateful for what I have, rather than what I don't have. I can be grateful and accept my addictions for making me the person I am today, rather than blaming them.

Today, I *am* grateful.

141. 73 DAYS CLEAN & SOBER

I'm a 15-year-old girl and I'm an alcoholic and addict. This is new for me to say with 73 days in the Program. I started drinking when I was eight. My dad gave me sips from his beer, and I liked how it tasted and how it made me feel. I'd sneak it when he got wasted. My parents got divorced when I was nine and I lived with my mom and my older sister in a pretty nasty-looking house.

My mother worked a lot during the night. My sister was four years older than I was, so she went out with high school guys and I was left on my own until my mom came home. I never got any attention, so I got it through neighbor boys. So there's me, Miss Flirt on the block. I first used pot about that time and tried to get high every day. My first time was with a couple of friends behind a garbage dump. From then on, I loved it, so I kept doing it. I never had to pay for it. I did some bad things to get it. I never liked myself or anyone else.

By the time I was 13, I was having major problems with my mom and my sister. Sometimes my mom and I would get on the floor and beat each other until the cops came.

I was having other problems and hanging around the wrong people four or five years older than I was. So I decided to move out and live with my father. I thought if I got away from my mom and those friends, I wouldn't have problems.

At my dad's and the new school, guess what? I found the crowd who drank and did drugs. I tried to get loaded before school, after school, any time I could get my hands on it. I would sit with friends, and smoke a bowl or two. Friday nights were the best. We would go to an old shack and smoke, drink, and drop acid and other drugs that people did. We never went anywhere; we just sat. Then one night an older guy walked me home through the woods, raped me and left me there. When I got home, I took a shower for an hour, I felt so dirty. I never told my mom or dad.

I moved back to my mom's because things were getting bad. I was making the problems worse. My mom and I didn't get along. She'd piss me off; I'd beat her up. I was so screwed up I didn't know whether I was going left, right, down or up. So my mom, behind my back, was calling around for a drug and rehab place. She found one for young people, and I went, kicking and screaming all the way.

I learned a lot in treatment. I found out other people my age have similar problems and how I can deal with my own. I have 73 days clean and sober. I went dancing the other night at a clean and sober club with my sponsor and danced until 1:00 a.m. I've gone to a lot of meetings and have had fun going bowling and doing other stuff without drugs and alcohol. There's *lots* of things to do in sobriety that are more beneficial than using.

I know I'm pretty new to this way of life and I'm probably on a pink cloud, but that's O.K. I'm going to try my best and stick with it. I don't want to be abused or abuse anyone any more, especially me. I don't want to be in blackouts, passed out, or overdose. I want to remember what I did the night before. I'm through wrecking my life or winding up with AIDS or some other disease that can *never* go away. So stay clean and sober. I need your help.

142. PRAYER AND MEDITATION

We're told that trying to pray *is* praying. "Oh, God, help me! If you get me out of this mess, I'll never screw up again." This was our favorite prayer before we entered the Program. We were always bargaining with God.

We have learned new prayers and a new way to talk and listen to our Higher Power. We are seeking God's will for us. Many of us had to learn *how* to pray. We began with very simple prayers: "God, help me know Your will for me." "Thank you, God, for helping me today."

We learn that prayer helps us with our overdependence on people, places, and things by giving us the insight and strength to rearrange our priorities. Prayer doesn't change God, but it changes those who pray.

Today in our prayers, we seek our Higher Power's will for us. We no longer bargain with God.

Prayer is seeking answers and direction in life. Meditation is listening for answers from a Higher Power and developing the faith within us to accept those answers. Reflection is finding ways to change the answers we get from prayer and meditation into *action*.

Reflection is understanding how to use the Twelve Steps. It is not snap judgment. It asks us to think of the pros and cons of our possible choices and to understand what directions we will take to give us the best results.

The progress of spirituality from prayer to meditation to reflection is active, not passive. It is taking part in the joy of putting the results of prayer and meditation into action.

We have learned through times of quiet reflection to work into our lives the answers our Higher Power has given us as a result of our prayer and meditation.

143. WHAT IF ...

At times during our recovery, we may ask ourselves those questions, "What if ... ," "Yeah, but ... ," and "If only ... ." We may wonder "what if" I had kept drinking? We may think "yeah, but I'm only 16 years old—I can't be an addict." Or "if only I could try it all over again." All these questions are legitimate ones, and sometimes they can be answered. Other times they may be dangerous to keep thinking about. We may begin to question our recovery and if we really belong in the Program. Sometimes it helps if we change the words around a little bit—like "what if I didn't make it to this Program?"

144. A TALK WITH MY HIGHER POWER

What an order, I can't go through with it!

And a small, quiet voice said: *Be still and know that I am God.*

But God, you just don't understand, I am so alone and so very afraid.

Somewhere in my heart I heard: *I will not give you any more than you can handle.*

In my terror I screamed, I am not as capable as you think I am! Inside I am very small and very young. Oh God, I am so alone.

Again, a peaceful loving voice replied: *You have never been alone and you are not alone now. If you let me in, I will walk with you.*

I am too afraid, I cried; my heart hurts, and I just don't know what to do anymore. I put out my hand and no one was there. Oh God, I am so alone.

A gentle voice replied: *Putting out your hand is not enough. You must reach out with your whole being: your heart, soul, and mind. I will hold you in your fear and I will teach you past your youth.*

I am afraid, my God, that if I do this you will go away. I fall on my face and make so many mistakes. You may not love me if I let go completely.

A warmth and peace beyond my understanding filled my heart and mind. And I began to understand I didn't have to be alone if I didn't really want to be.

Very softly, very quietly, I heard: *The lesson isn't over until you've learned it completely. If you fail, if you fall, I will catch you. Ask for me and I will come. You only have to ask. You never have to be alone again. In times of sadness, I will send you comfort; when you are alone, I will send someone; in times of tremendous turmoil, I will grant you the gift of peace. Still, you must ask, even when you don't believe. And continue to reach out to others, for they are as scared and alone as you feel now.*

*Life is difficult, but if you seek me and follow what
I say to your heart, then for any pain you live
through I will bless you with joy. For every time you
reach out in blind faith, I will grant you peace within
yourself and with others.*

And I came to believe that a power greater
than myself, God, could and would restore me to
sanity. What I couldn't do for myself, God had. So
I reached out my heart, soul and mind to God. Thy
will, not mine, be done. Amen.

145. THE MOST IMPORTANT THING

Being young and in recovery wasn't always
easy in the "old days." Young people were few and
hard to come by. It wasn't easy to be accepted as an
alcoholic or drug addict by the old-timers. There
weren't meetings that were specifically for young
people. Young people weren't included in clean
and sober activities.

Today, times have changed. There are meetings for young people, chaired and organized by
young people. There is a national organization for
young people. There are activities planned by
young people, for young people. There are clean
and sober dance clubs for young people. There are

more and more young people involved in service work. Now there are treatment centers for young people.

Today there are places to go for young people, places that are clean and sober. We can have fun without booze and drugs. We can stay out late and not get in trouble with parents or police. We can be honest about our destination. We can wake up feeling good about ourselves, not worrying or forgetting what we did the night before or who we did "it" with. We can have fun in sobriety. We can be involved in the Fellowship. We can be accepted by our fellow members as an equal. Recovery is rewarding and fun.

146. SLOGANS

1. Easy Does It
2. First Things First
3. Live and Let Live
4. But for the Grace of God
5. Think . . . Think . . . Think
6. One Day at a Time
7. Let Go and Let God
8. K.I.S.S.—Keep It Simple, Stupid
9. Act As If . . .

10. This Too Shall Pass
11. Expect A Miracle
12. I Can't . . . God Can . . . I Think I'll Let Him
13. If It Works . . . Don't Fix It
14. Keep Coming Back . . . It Works If You Work It, It Won't If You Don't
15. Stick With the Winners
16. Identify Don't Compare
17. Recovery Is A Journey, Not A Destination
18. H.O.W. = Honesty, Openmindedness, Willingness
19. Poor Me . . . Poor Me . . . Pour Me Another Drink
20. To Thine Own Self Be True
21. I Came; I Came To; I Came To Believe
22. Live In The NOW
23. If God Seems Far Away, Who Moved?
24. Turn It Over
25. Utilize, Don't Analyze
26. Nothing Is So Bad, Relapse Won't Make It Worse
27. We Are Only As Sick As Our Secrets
28. Drop The Rock
29. Be Part Of The Solution, Not The Problem
30. Sponsors: Have One—Use One—Be One
31. I Can't Handle It God; You Take Over

32. Keep An Open Mind
33. It Works—It Really Does!
34. Willingness Is The Key
35. Don't Quit—Surrender
36. Hugs, Not Drugs
37. Clean and Serene
38. No Pain . . . No Gain
39. Go For It
40. Principles Before Personalities
41. Do It Sober
42. Screw Guilt
43. Just For Today
44. Sober 'n Crazy
45. Pass It On
46. N.U.T.S. = Not Using the Steps
47. S.O.B.E.R. = Son Of A Bitch, Everything's Real
48. Before You Say: I Can't . . . Say: I'll Try
49. Don't Quit 5 Minutes Before The Miracle Happens
50. Some Of Us Are Sicker Than Others
51. We're All Here Because We're Not All There
52. Addiction Is An Equal Opportunity Destroyer
53. Gratitude Is The Attitude
54. H.A.L.T. = Don't Get Too Hungry, Angry, Lonely, or Tired

55. Another Friend Of Bill W's
56. God Is Never Late
57. Have A Good Day Unless You've Made Other Plans
58. Shit Happens
59. E.G.O. = Edging God Out
60. 90 Meetings 90 Days
61. You Are Not Alone
62. Wherever You Go, There You Are
63. Don't Drink, Read The Big Book, And Go To Meetings
64. Use The 24-Hour Plan
65. Make Use Of Telephone Therapy
66. Stay in Recovery For Yourself
67. Look For Similarities Rather Than Differences
68. Remember Your Last Drunk
69. Remember That Addiction Is Incurable, Progressive, and Fatal
70. Try Not To Place Conditions On Your Recovery
71. When All Else Fails Follow Directions
72. Count Your Blessings
73. Share Your Happiness
74. Respect The Anonymity of Others
75. Pain Is Optional

76. Let Go Of Old Ideas
77. Try To Replace Guilt With Gratitude
78. What Goes Around, Comes Around
79. Change Is A Process, Not An Event
80. Take The Cotton Out Of Your Ears And Put It In Your Mouth
81. Call Your Sponsor Before, Not After, You Take The First Drink
82. Sick And Tired Of Being Sick And Tired
83. It's The First Drink That Gets You Drunk
84. To Keep It, You Have To Give It Away
85. P.L.O.M. = Poor Little Old Me
86. Remember Happiness And Serenity Are An Inside Job
87. Any Addict Clean Is A Miracle
88. Take What You Can Use And Leave The Rest
89. We Demand Less And Give More
90. Believe In God Or Be God
91. If Only . . .
92. Help Is Only A Phone Call Away
93. Around The Program Or In The Program?
94. You Can't Give Away What You Don't Have
95. One Drink Is Too Many And A Thousand Not Enough
96. Welcome And "Keep Coming Back"

97. Anger Is But One Letter Away From Danger
98. Courage To Change . . .
99. Easy Does It, But Do It
100. Bring The Body And The Mind Will Follow

147. PRAYER OF ST. FRANCIS ASSISI

Lord, make me an instrument
of Your peace!
Where there is hatred, let me sow love.
Where there is injury, pardon.
Where there is doubt, faith.
Where there is despair, hope.
Where there is darkness, light.
Where there is sadness, joy.

O Divine Master,
Grant that I may not so much seek
To be consoled as to console.
To be understood as to understand.
To be loved as to love.
For it is in giving
that we receive.
It is in pardoning
that we are pardoned.
It is in dying
that we are born to eternal life.

148. SERENITY PRAYER

God grant me the serenity
To accept the things I cannot change;
The courage to change the things I can;
And the wisdom to know the difference.

Living one day at a time;
Enjoying one moment at a time;
Accepting hardship as the pathway to peace;

Taking, as He did,
This sinful world as it is,
Not as I would have it;
Trusting that He will
Make all things right
If I surrender to His Will;

That I may be
reasonably happy in this life,
And supremely happy with Him
Forever in the next.

149. SANSKRIT PROVERB

Look to this day,
For it is life,
The very life of life.
In its brief course lies all
The realities and verities of existence,
The bliss of growth,
The splendor of action,
The glory of power.
For yesterday is but a dream,
And tomorrow is only a vision.
But today, well lived,
Makes every yesterday
A dream of happiness
And every tomorrow
A vision of hope.
Look well, therefore, to this day.

150. TO BE PRAYER

O Lord, I ain't what I ought to be,
And I ain't what I want to be,
And I ain't what I'm going to be,
But O Lord, I thank You
That I ain't what I used to be.

INDEX

The Twelve Steps Of Alcoholics Anonymous

1. We admitted we were powerless over alcohol—that our lives had become unmanageable.
2. Came to believe that a Power greater than ourselves could restore us to sanity.
3. Made a decision to turn our will and our lives over to the care of God *as we understood Him*.
4. Made a searching and fearless moral inventory of ourselves.
5. Admitted to God, to ourselves, and to another human being the exact nature of our wrongs.
6. Were entirely ready to have God remove all these defects of character.
7. Humbly asked Him to remove our shortcomings.
8. Made a list of all persons we had harmed, and became willing to make amends to them all.
9. Made direct amends to such people wherever possible, except when to do so would injure them or others.
10. Continued to take personal inventory and when we were wrong promptly admitted it.
11. Sought through prayer and meditation to improve our conscious contact with God *as we understood Him*, praying only for knowledge of His will for us and the power to carry that out.
12. Having had a spiritual awakening as the result of these steps, we tried to carry this message to alcoholics, and to practice these principles in all our affairs.

The Twelve Steps reprinted with permission of A.A. World Services, Inc., New York, New York.

Distributed by . . .

HAZELDEN INFORMATION & EDUCATIONAL SERVICES
P.O. BOX 176
15251 Pleasant Valley Road
Center City, MN 55012-0176

HAZELDEN®

For price and order information, or a free catalog,
please call our Telephone Representatives.

1-800-328-0098
(Toll Free. U.S., Canada, and the Virgin Islands)

1-651-213-4000
(Outside the U.S., and Canada)

1-651-213-4590
(24-Hour FAX)

http://www.Hazelden.org
(World Wide Web site on Internet)